The 50 Commands of JESUS

To Know and Obey
(TKO)

The 50 Commands of Jesus
Copyright © 2023 by JD Biggerstaff

Published in the United States of America
ISBN   Paperback: 979-8-89091-143-8
ISBN   eBook: 979-8-89091-144-5

All rights reserved. No part of this publication may be reproduced, stored in a retrieval system or transmitted in any way by any means, electronic, mechanical, photocopy, recording or otherwise without the prior permission of the author except as provided by USA copyright law.

The opinions expressed by the author are not necessarily those of ReadersMagnet, LLC.

ReadersMagnet, LLC
10620 Treena Street, Suite 230 | San Diego, California, 92131 USA
1.619. 354. 2643 | www.readersmagnet.com

Book design copyright © 2023 by ReadersMagnet, LLC. All rights reserved.

Cover design by Ericka Obando
Interior design by Don De Guzman

The 50 Commands of Jesus
To Know and Obey
(TKO)

"I hear ya' cluckin', but I don't see no eggs." That's what my boss said to me years ago when I was giving him reasons [excuses] for not completing an important assignment on time. Looking back, I should have prioritized better and completed my assignment in a timely manner. I allowed various distractions to bog me down and I was not as diligent as I should have been in completing my boss's directive. My boss was somewhat gracious and restrained as he lectured me on the importance of "obedience, diligence and timeliness" concerning his directives and assignments.

Now, imagine for a moment that your boss is Jesus of Nazareth, the Christ. (Actually, He is our boss, the BIG One.)

Christians often call Christ Jesus their "Lord and Savior." Many trust in Jesus as their Savior enough to keep them out of Hell, but few trust Him enough as the Lord of their lives to follow His teachings and commands. Too few Christians even know the commands of Jesus much less obey them. FYI: There are about 50 commands of Christ recorded in the Four Gospels. You can easily find different lists on the Internet with different numbers of commands, but the list I use here has 50.

How many of these commands do you know and are obedient to do them? Are the words in red important to you? They should be if you claim to be a Christian. Scripture tells us in multiple places that our obedience is more important [to God] than our sacrifice. [1 Samuel 15:22, Proverbs 21:3, Jeremiah 7:21-23, Matthew 12:7]

We are also told in scripture to worship God in spirit and in truth. One of the best ways to remain in the Spirit of Truth is to make a lifestyle of studying the Word of God. That includes reading, studying, meditating on, declaring and living what Jesus' words tell us to do. Don't forget the importance of daily praise, prayer and thanksgiving. A great place to start worshiping in spirit and truth is to learn and act on [be obedient to] the commands of Jesus – especially if you consider Him your Lord and Savior.

Jesus is quoted in the Books of John and Luke:

John 15:14,	*"You are my friends if you do whatever I command you."*
John 14:15,	*"If you love me, obey my commands."*
John 14:23,	*"If anyone loves me, he will obey my teaching."*
John 14:24,	*"He who does not love me will not obey my teaching."*
John 3:36,	*"… whoever does not obey the Son shall not see life, but the wrath of God remains on him."*
Luke 6:46	*"Why do you call me 'Lord Lord' and do not do what I tell you?"*
Luke 11: 28	*"Blessed are those who hear the Word of God and keep it."*

Jesus told Thomas in John 20:29 that he believed because he had seen Him; then Jesus went on to say: *"blessed are those who have not seen and yet have believed."* Jesus' promise of blessings applies to us today who would believe in Him without seeing Him in person.

There is a summary of those promised blessings near the end of this book. For more than two centuries Jesus has kept His promises to those Believers who store up [know and saturate] His words in their hearts and minds. Jesus' teachings have changed the world and its history for the better. Most often, that change is one life at a time. As you begin to focus on and abide [rest, remain, relax in, trust, obey] in Jesus' words, you will begin to experience their supernatural life-changing power in your life. You will begin to see blessings manifest beyond what is humanly possible. Joy and peace from God will be yours as you love the Son and obey His words.

People measure their love for other people by their feelings, which are often fleeting, fickle and fluctuate based on circumstances. The love that Christ Jesus values is based on our obedience to His Words. The Words of Jesus reflect the will of God. Sadly, many people who profess to believe in Jesus know very little of His teachings and do very little to obey them. Our obedience to Jesus' commands expresses our love for Him, our trust in Him and our faith in Him. Those teachings and commands give us the power and guidance to help us overcome the many trials of this life in a joyful peaceful manner. They provide light in a dark world. Our obedience will lift us up rather than weigh us down. We please God when we obey the words of the Son. We should make pleasing God [rather than man] an important part of our daily life.

In John 15:16 Jesus tells us that our lives should produce good fruit. *"…I chose you, and appointed you that you would go and bear fruit, and that your fruit would remain."* We often crowd our schedules with things that don't make a lasting difference in our lives; thus, we have wasted time that could have been better served in producing good fruit. Know that time is one of our most limited resources. The Bible says a man will be known by his fruit [what he does that blesses other people]. If you obey the commands of Jesus, you cannot help but to produce good fruit.

We are also told [commanded] to go and make disciples [followers] of Christ Jesus. [Mathew 28:19-20]. This is often called the Great Commission. If you take this command seriously and are obedient to do it, realize [sadly] that some people simply won't believe no matter what you say or do. Everyone is called [invited, summoned] to Jesus, but not everyone will accept Him and be allowed to stay. See the Parable of the Wedding Feast.

Jesus told his disciples that most people would not believe [even after hearing Him speak and seeing His miracles] because they were not called to be His sheep. He explained that His sheep will hear His voice, come to Him and be obedient to his teachings. We who are called to be His sheep should continue to be His witness by sowing His words and doing works of righteousness wherever we go. Never miss an opportunity to talk about the Gospel of Jesus as you help make disciples. Don't get frustrated, but know that not everyone will accept Jesus' invitation to be His sheep. Do your part to be Jesus' ambassador on earth and let God do His part in calling those whom He has chosen to receive, believe in and obey the Son.

This short book presents the 50 commands of Christ Jesus in a straightforward easy-to-read manner to help the reader learn them. There is one section for each of the 50 commands with the Words of Jesus in red from the Amplified Bible. These scripture verses are followed by a short discussion and commentary on what a Christian should know and attempt to do [behaviorally] to be obedient to that command. In the Bible, many important points and themes are stated multiple times in multiple places. Some sections of this book list additional references to a command of Jesus found in other places outside of the Four Gospels.

People often think of the Commands in the Bible as rules that will restrict their life and rob them of joy, happiness and pleasure. In reality, it is quite the contrary. Our obedience to Biblical principles opens the floodgates for God's blessings to pour out, chase us down and overtake us. Those blessings include peace, joy, prosperity, freedom from oppression of the enemy, forgiveness, right standing with God, and most importantly our Salvation [Heaven].

Many people want to know the will of God for their lives and they have a heart's desire to be within the will of God. It begins by actively seeking God's will with all your heart. You will find the will of God in Jesus' words every time you read them. Take time and make it a priority to study, know and obey the words and commands of Christ Jesus. In John 15:7 Jesus tells us "If you abide [stay, dwell, rest, relax, remain] in Me, and my words abide in you, ask whatever you wish it will be done for you [by My Father]." This is a powerful promise from our Lord.

At the end of the section for each command, you the reader can self-assess your level of obedience to the command of Jesus in terms of

Near the end of this book, there is even a section on how you can self-assess [score] your overall level of obedience to Jesus' commands. This section provides suggestions on how to establish improvement goals, for those who are so inclined. [called to be His sheep]

Remember that the Christian life is a never-ending journey to become more Christ-like over time. As human beings, our obedience will never be perfect, but our life's direction should be determined by learning, living and obeying the commands of Jesus. Hopefully, this book will help you in your earthly journey toward your eternal home.

THE 50 COMMANDS OF JESUS

"God responds to those who seek him diligently, not casually."

The 50 Commands of Jesus: (all scripture references taken from the Amplified Bible)

1. Repent [stop sinning]

Matt 4:17 From that time Jesus began to preach and say, *"Repent [change your inner self - your old way of thinking, regret past sins, live your life in a way that proves repentance; seek God's purpose for your life], for the kingdom of heaven is at hand."*

Luke 13:3 *"I tell you, no; but unless you repent [change your old way of thinking, turn from your sinful ways and live changed lives] you will all likewise perish."*

Commentary on What to Know and Do:

Know that the very first word of Jesus in his public life [as recorded in Matthew 4:17] was the word *"Repent."* Literally, repent means to turn your life around and go in a different direction [without the sin(s) of your past].

True repentance is a process that would commonly follow these steps:

- Be honest with yourself and determine what sin(s) need to be eliminated from your life
- Develop a "Godly sorrow" for your sin(s) [sorrow for what you did]
- Confess your sin(s) to God and ask for forgiveness
- Ask the Holy Spirit to help you make the needed changes from the inside out
- Go a different and better direction in your life
- Don't repeat your sin(s)
- Go forward constructively in your life without guilt and shame

John the Baptist's role in life was to herald the coming of the Messiah [Jesus]. His best-known message to people as he preached in the wilderness was *"Repent, for the kingdom of God is near."* (Matthew 3:2) John was called "the Baptist" because his practice was to water-baptize those who responded to his message to confess and to sincerely repent of their sins. John also taught a secondary message and warned that **judgement** was at hand. In Matthew 4:10 John said *"Already the axe [of God's judgement] is swinging toward the root of the trees, therefore every tree that does not produce good fruit is cut down and thrown into the fire."*

Remember that God judges sin and there are consequences of your sins. *You do reap what you sow* [good or bad]. The consequences of your sin(s) are not always immediate because God loves you and patiently gives you time to change [repent]. Know that the consequences of your sins can carry on to your family through generational curses to the third and fourth generations [Ex 5:6, Ex 20:5, Ex 34:9, Numbers 14:18 Deut. 5:9]. Your sins rarely affect just you.

For example: The sins of King David [sexual immorality, adultery and murder] opened up a spiritual doorway that allowed sexual sin and murder into the lives of his children with many negative consequences. You would do well to learn from these Biblical lessons about the impact of sin.

David's first born son, Amnon, lusted after and raped his half sister Tamar. David's third oldest son Absalom murdered Amnon in revenge for raping his sister. The child born from David's and Bathsheba's sexual immorality died shortly after birth. Later in David's reign, Absalom tried to kill his father to take over his throne. Absalom led a great civil war that killed many thousands of people. David's sins were costly and caused serious fatal consequences for thousands of people, even beyond his family.

There is some good news about **repentance** in David's story. He and Bathsheba repented and were forgiven by God. After they were legitimately married, God blessed their union and they had a second son who lived and was named Soloman. Soloman became a great king, exceedingly rich and was chosen to build the Temple. Under Soloman's reign there was great peace and prosperity in Judea.

Note: Many people are only "sorry" when they have to suffer the consequence(s) of their sins. [Much like a child who is only sorry they got caught rather than truly sorry for what they did]. We need to view our sins as "a stench in the nostrils of God" and be truly sorry for them [have a godly sorrow] prior to confessing them to God and asking for His forgiveness.

As Christians, we know that the sins of unbelievers are judged and lead to eternal hell and damnation. The greatest sin of an unbeliever is that they rejected the grace, mercy, forgiveness and salvation offered by Lord Jesus. First John 1:9 tells us *"if we confess our sins, He is faithful and just to forgive our sins."* Know that the "unrepented sins" of the believer are also judged. You should make it a priority in your life to repent [stop conscious sinning] immediately, before it is too late and the consequences lead to destruction.

As a practical suggestion, list your top three sins and rank-order them. Write out your plan to purge them from your life. This plan would often include identifying the bad thoughts and behaviors you must eliminate and then determining the good thoughts and behaviors you should substitute. A Christian counselor might suggest you write down [document] on a sheet of paper each of your sins you have chosen work on. Once you have mastered that sin, rip that sheet up and throw it away to signify your victory over it and to receive God's forgiveness. As you have successfully conquered [repented of] these first three sins, keep going on to the next three until you have repented of all conscious sin in your life.

We, as human beings, have a very limited ability to change anything in our lives. In Matthew 19:25 the disciples asked Jesus "who can be saved from the wrath of God?" In Matthew 19:26 Jesus looked at them and replied, *"With people [as far as it depends on them] it is impossible, but with God all things are possible."* God can set us free from the many sins in our lives [deadly addictions, degrading lifestyles, anger, violence, hatred, unforgiveness, judgementalness, greed, adultery, lust, abortion, etc.] if we ask Him and allow Him. That is where our Helper, the Holy Spirit, comes in. He can change us from the inside out if we seek Him, surrender to Him and allow

Him to work in our lives. Lasting true repentance requires the help of the Holy Spirit.

My obedience level to this command is:

2. Let not your heart be troubled [worry and fear]

John 14:1 *"DO NOT let your heart be troubled [afraid, cowardly]. Believe [confidently] in God and trust in Him, [have faith, hold onto it, rely on it, keep going and] believe also in Me."*

John 14:27 *"The person who has My commandments and keeps them is one who [really] loves Me; and whoever [really] loves Me will be loved by my Father, and I will love him and reveal Myself to him [I will make myself real to him].*

John 16:33 *"I have told you these things, so that in Me you may have [perfect] peace. In the world you have tribulation and distress and suffering, but be courageous [be confident, be undaunted, be filled with joy]; I have overcome the world. [My conquest is accomplished, My victory abiding.]"*

Matt 6:25-26 *"Therefore I tell you, stop being worried or anxious [perpetually uneasy, distracted] about your life., as to what you will eat or what you will drink; nor about your body, as to what you will wear. Is life not more than food and the body more than clothing?"*

Phil 4:6-7   Do not be anxious or worried about anything, but in everything [every circumstance and situation] by prayer and petition with thanksgiving, continue to make your [specific] requests known to God. And the peace of God [that peace that reassures the heart, that peace] which transcends all understanding, [that peace which] stands guard over your hearts and your minds in Christ Jesus [is yours].

Commentary on What to Know and Do:

Jesus' command *"let not your heart be troubled"* is one of the best known and often quoted of His commands. In context, Jesus had told a crowd plus His disciples that He would soon be crucified and that one of His disciples would betray Him. [John 12 and 13.] Obviously, this was extremely upsetting news to His followers. He went on to communicate that He would leave them to *"prepare the place"* in heaven for them and that He was not going to abandon them because He would soon send His Holy Spirit to be their Helper, Teacher and Comforter. Rather than leaving them destitute, He explained that His death would bring about two specific blessings [heaven and the Holy Spirit]. Jesus meant this to be an antidote for the not-so-good news He had just shared about the ugly and evil circumstances of His trial and death.

While the circumstances have changed, Jesus' admonition still applies to us today. You should not let your heart be troubled by worry or anxiety about Jesus' plan and care for you. Rest in the salvation that Jesus provides and rely on the Holy Spirit to help you navigate the fallen world around you.

Be at peace and do not be afraid. There is no need to struggle with so many worries. Sociologists tell us that about 94% of the things we worry about never happen and of the 6% that do happen, only about 3% are within our control. Focus on the 3% within your control and turn the rest over to the Lord to fight your battles. Be still and know the strength and salvation of the Lord.

Know that Jesus promises to bring a supernatural peace to believers that defies the world view of peace. Know that only Jesus can calm the storms of your life and bring you peace in spite of your circumstances. Because of Jesus' great love for you, you do not need to be troubled and worry if you will only abide in His words, obey them, trust and depend on Him. To trust and depend on Jesus, you must first learn and believe that God/Jesus really loves you and wants to provide for you and bless you. Know that God is honored when you depend on Him and come to Him humbly with your needs and concerns.

Jesus said the world would always be full of trouble, but he said to take heart because He has overcome the world. Take Jesus' yoke upon you and let Him carry your burdens. He will do that for you. When you cast your burdens on the Holy Spirit [the Christ within], you go free to enjoy God's peace and blessings. His plans and will for your life are to bless and prosper you. Trust in God's great love, mercy and grace for his creation [you]. Focus on Jesus and not your problems because He is the problem-solver. He will provide for those who put their faith in Him. You can trust Him for everything you need. Jesus said in John 10:10 ... *"I came that they* [you and me] *have and enjoy life, and have it in abundance* [to the full, till it overflows]. Put faith over fear. Realize that worry and fear are acts of disobedience to this command of Jesus.

A practical way to cast your burden involves making a declarative statement like this out loud:

"Today, I cast my burden(s) of _____ on the Christ within, and I am freed to enjoy _____. (Fill in the blanks for your specific needs and circumstances.)

As a born-again believer, know that you are adopted into the family of God and become a joint heir to His kingdom. You are an adopted child of the most High God which entitles you to all His benefits. God owns it all and He is not financially or resource limited. Believe and trust that God loves you and wants to bless and provide for you. Realize that worry is unnecessary because of God's great love. You are to obediently work with the Holy Spirit and know that your efforts [not to worry] will be energized and divinely directed by God Himself. When God directs you to do anything, He will empower you to do it. When you listen to Jesus and believe Him, deliverance from the world's troubles and supernatural peace will begin to manifest and become a reality in your life. Rejoice and be happy in the peace and comfort of the Lord. Do not let your heart be troubled.

My obedience level to this command is:

3. Follow Me

Matt 4:19   And He said to them, *"Follow Me [as My disciples, accepting Me as your Master and Teacher walking the same path in life that I walk], and I will make you fishers of men."*

Commentary on What to Know and Do:

Follow Jesus' examples and learn from Him. Be mentored by Jesus by learning his words, thoughts, choices and actions in His life. Then emulate Him based on what you learn from Him. Know and obey His commands by applying them in your daily life. A good principle to guide your life in making decisions is to ask yourself 'what would Jesus do? (WWJD)' The Holy Spirit is your teacher who will help bring the words of Jesus to your recollection at the proper times if you ask and allow Him to do so.

Make Jesus your Master and Teacher, your Lord and Savior. Become a disciple [follower] of Jesus and know that true disciples help make other disciples. Jesus told his disciples they would become "fishers of men." Are you a "fisher of men" who leads others to the Lord and helps build other disciples [followers of Jesus]? Do you know and follow the teachings of Jesus? Do you make Him the Lord of your life?

My obedience level to this command is:

4. Rejoice [be happy if others put you down]

Mathew 5:10   *"Blessed [comforted by inner peace and God's love] are those who are persecuted for doing that which is morally right, for theirs is the kingdom of heaven* [both now and forever].

Matt 5:11-12   *"Blessed are you when people insult you and persecute you, and falsely say all kinds of evil things against you because of Me. Be glad and exceedingly joyful, for your reward in heaven is great* [absolutely inexhaustible]; *for this is the same way they persecuted the prophets who were before you."*

2 Cor 12:10   So I [Paul] am well pleased with weakness, with insults, with distresses, with persecutions, and with difficulties, for the sake of Christ; for when I am weak [in human strength], then I am strong [truly able, truly powerful, truly drawing on God's strength].

James 1:2-4   Consider it nothing but joy, my brothers and sisters when you fall into various trials. Be assured that the testing of your faith [through experience] produces endurance [leading to spiritual maturity and inner peace]. And let endurance have its perfect result and do a thorough work, so that you may be perfect and completely developed [in your faith], lacking in nothing.

<u>Commentary on What to Know and Do:</u>

If someone mocks or harasses you because of your faith, then be glad. Almost anyone who chooses to call themselves a Christian will face various kinds of opposition over time. This opposition can range the gamut from intellectual rejection to physical torture and death [in some parts of the world].

Know and be glad that there is a great reward in Heaven for those who suffer "for righteousness, for Christ." [followers of Jesus]. Throughout history the speakers of unwelcomed truths [the prophets] were persecuted, and you will be persecuted too as a disciple of Christ

Jesus. Be strong in your faith and be joyful knowing that great eternal rewards await you. Delight in your trials and persecutions knowing that when you are weak, that is when Christ is strong in you and for you. Be joyful knowing that trials in your life produce perseverance plus great eternal rewards. We are to praise and glorify God in ALL circumstances.

When difficulties come your way, focus your attention on **"what"** you should learn and do rather than **"why"** that difficulty has happened. Human nature often wants to know why. Many times you will never know why something bad or difficult has happened. The sooner you learn "what" you are supposed to learn, to do and move on, the sooner the impact of the difficulty will subside.

My obedience level to this command is:

5. Let your light shine

Matthew 5:16 *"Let your light shine before men in such a way they may see your good deeds and moral excellence, and* [recognize and honor] *glorifying your Father who is in heaven."*

Commentary on What to Know and Do:

Become known for your goodness to others. Let your life light shine so all people can see your good works and praise/glorify your Father in Heaven. Walk in love, kindness, forgiveness, and mercy. Strive to become renown for your goodness to others. Always do the right things right so your life is a living example for all to see. This glorifies and honors the Father.

An important principle in spiritual law is that "like energies attract like energies." If you think, say and do good things, you will begin to attract good things and circumstances back to you over time. The opposite is true if you think, say and do bad, negative and evil things, that is what you will attract into your life. This spiritual law is the driving force in the Biblical principle of *sowing and reaping* [giving and receiving].

Know that God's blessings follow you in this life as well as await you in your next life for doing good godly things that glorify the Father. Choose to be such a bright *light* in a *dark* world that it is obvious to others to whom you belong and to whom you glorify [giving praise and honor].

My obedience level to this command is:

6. Honor God's law

Mathew 5:17-19 *"Do not think that I came to do away with or undo the Law* [of Moses, the 10 Commandments] *or the writings of the prophets; I did not come to destroy but to fulfill. For I assure you most solemnly say to you, until heaven and earth pass away, not the smallest letter or stroke* [of the pen] *will pass from the Law until all things* [which foreshadow it] *are accomplished. So whoever breaks one of the least of these commandments, and teaches others to do the same, will be called least* [important] *in the kingdom of heaven; but whoever practices and teaches them, he will be called great in the kingdom of heaven.*

Commentary on What to Know and Do:

Know that Jesus came to fulfill the Law, not abolish or change it. The 50 commands of Jesus expand on the original 10 Commandments, often called the Law of Moses. We are to follow the commandments of the Law and teach others to do so as well. It helps to know what those commandments are so you can attempt to follow them. There are great rewards in Heaven for doing this. You will be called 'great' in the Kingdom of God.

Also know that no human can be perfect in following the Law. No one is able, but do your best to be obedient and try. The purpose of the Law is to show you your shortcomings and make you aware of your utter dependence on God. Do not ignore God's Laws or lead others in not following the Laws and commandments. There are eternal penalties if you lead others astray and you will be called 'least' in the Kingdom of God.

My obedience level to this command is:

7. Reconcile with your enemies

Matthew 5:23-25   *"...if your brother has something* [such as a grievance or legitimate complaint] *against you, leave your offering there at the alter and go. First make peace with your brother, and then come and present your offering. Come to terms quickly* [at your earliest opportunity] *with your opponent at law while you are with him on your way* [to court], *so that your opponent does not hand you over to the judge, and the judge to the guard, and you are thrown into prison."*

Commentary on What to Know and Do:

If you realize you are in conflict with another person, go and make a serious attempt to reconcile with them, even if you believe they are in the wrong. Jesus essentially commands you to make the first move in restoring broken or damaged relationships.

Don't bother coming to God with your prayers before you have attempted to heal the broken relationships with people. This means to proactively attempt to mend broken relationships prior to bringing your prayers, offerings, or petitions to God for your needs/wants.

God will not hear you because of the hardness of your heart [anger, bitterness, resentment, a grudge, revenge, unforgiveness, etc.]. Also, go and attempt to reconcile with anyone you are in conflict with before going to court. Be a peace-maker.

Often you must decide to forgive someone in your heart before you attempt to reconcile a damaged or broken relationship. It's not enough to simply think forgiveness; Jesus exhorts you to go in person to seek reconciliation. Forgive them in your heart, and then go in person and attempt to remove the barriers between you. If your efforts are rejected, you will not be judged by their response. That sin of unforgiveness is on them not you. Know that forgiveness is critical for both parties [you and the other person] to be free to move on in life.

My obedience level to this command is:

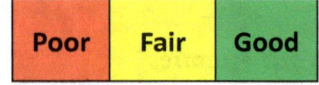

8. Do not commit adultery or lust

Matthew 5:27-29   *"you have heard it said, 'YOU SHALL NOT COMMIT ADULRTY'*; [Ex 20:14, Deut 5:18] *but I say to you that everyone who looks at a woman with lust for her has already committed adultery with her in his heart. If … makes you stumble and leads you to sin, tear it out and throw it away* [that is, remove yourself from the source of temptation]; *for it is better to lose one of the parts of your body, than for your whole body to be thrown into hell."*

Commentary on What to Know and Do:

Do not lust after or have relations with someone who is not your partner/spouse. You also commit adultery in your heart if you have a lustful eye. Resist temptation and do not let lust or sexual sin cast you into hell. Chose in advance to proactively flee and/or avoid a situation that you can reasonably anticipate being a temptation to you. Know that sexual sin is one of Satan's most powerful and successful weapons in attacking people. In today's digital world, on-line pornography has become one of Satan's modern weapons of attack [including the porn available on subscription television]. If you have fallen into sexual sin in the past, repent and change your ways going forward. We serve a God of grace and mercy. Ask the Holy Spirit for help in this battle.

Jesus shared some "hyperbolic wit" when he told his followers to cut off their hand or gouge out their eye if it helped them to keep from committing sins of lust and adultery. His real message is to be very proactive and aggressive in avoiding temptations and sin.

Okay. So, what do you do when you see someone who you find to be especially attractive physically? One of the first things to do is to thank and praise God that He has created such an attractive person [at least based on outward appearances]. Know that we humans will often have a sexual fantasy [even if only briefly] about such a person. Your goal at that time should be to move on from those sexual thoughts as quickly as possible so you do not linger and dwell on that person. When you linger and dwell on that fantasy you are drifting into the sin of lust. That person is not yours to gawk at. Consciously, shift your attention to something else [hopefully of a Godly nature, see Philippians 4:8] and move on about your day.

Shifting your thoughts is something of a skill that takes time and practice to develop. Don't forget to ask the Holy Spirit to help you develop this skill. He will help if you ask and allow Him to do so.

My obedience level to this command is:

9. Keep your word

Matthew 5:33-37 *"Again, you have heard that it was said to the men of old, 'YOU SHALL NOT MAKE FALSE VOWS, BUT YOU*

SHALL FULFILL YOUR VOWS TO THE LORD [AS A RELIGEUS DUTY].' *But I say to you, do not make an oath at all, either by heaven, for it is the throne of God or by the earth, for it is the footstool of His feet; or by Jerusalem, for it is THE CITY OF THE GREAT KING. Nor shall you make an oath by your head, for you are not able to make a single hair white or black. But let your statement be 'Yes, yes,' or 'No, no'* [a firm yes or no]; *anything more than that comes from the evil one."*

<u>Commentary on What to Know and Do:</u>

Do not swear any oaths at all. Do what you say you will, and do not make promises you will not or cannot keep. Fulfill to the Lord any vows you have made. Failing to do what you said you would do can fall under the sin of lying.

In your communication, let a simple YES or NO affirm the issue or deny the issue. Let your YES be YES and your NO be NO. A simple YES or NO is enough; anything beyond this comes from the "evil one."

Many people tend to give long-winded answers with many unnecessary qualifications even when they are asked a simple question. Three good, suggested responses to a question are "yes, no, or I don't know but I will find out and get back to you quickly." Then state qualifications [if you must] to fully answer the question. Avoid being guilty of providing TMI [too much information] when it is not called for. I once heard a politician say, "Blessed are the brief, for they shall be re-elected."

In life, it is cliched that trust is "hard to earn and easy to lose." You should strive to become so trustworthy and reliable that all you need to say is "yes" and those who know you [and know of you] will know that your word is your bond.

My obedience level to this command is:

10. Go above and beyond

Matthew 5:40-42   *If anyone wants to sue you and take your shirt, let him have your coat also* [for the Lord repays the offender]. *And whoever forces you to go one mile, go with him two. Give to him who asks of you and do not turn away from him who wants to borrow from you."*

Commentary on What to Know and Do:

Be willing to do more [above and beyond] than whatever someone asks of you and then do it cheerfully. Follow the path of generosity and practice non-resistance. This often requires you to put selfish pride aside and practice unselfish servanthood.

Know that in Biblical times under Roman law, a Roman soldier could require a local citizen to carry his armor for a mile. Jesus teaches us to do more than required by law [carry the armor two miles] and even do more than someone asks or expects. When you do this, you are sowing love and positive energies that will eventually come back to you under spiritual law. Jesus clearly taught that to be great in the Kingdom of God we should have a servant's heart and be willing to cheerfully serve others, usually with no expectation of anything in return. Going above and beyond puts your "greatness" into practice.

My obedience level to this command is:

11. Turn the other cheek and love your enemies

Matthew 5:39, 5:44   *"But I say to you, do not resist an evil person* [who insults you or violates your rights], *but whoever slaps you on the right cheek, turn the other to him also* [simply ignore insignificant insults or trivial losses and do not bother to retaliate-maintain your dignity, your self-respect, your poise].

"But I say to you, love [that is, unselfishly seek the best or higher good for] *your enemies, and pray for those who persecute you."*

Commentary on What to Know and Do:

Don't retaliate or take revenge on those who do you wrong. Don't repay evil for evil but trust in God's justice. This takes a lot of faith and patience. Be undisturbed and pray heart-felt blessings on your enemies and adversaries. Know that you will be the first to be blessed by God. His justice is always better than your revenge; however, God's timing for His justice may not always be the timing you would hope for.

The command to love and bless your enemies is an important aspect of Christianity that differs from almost every other belief system in the world, whether religious or secular. It defies common sense and the emotion of the human heart, but you are commanded by your Lord to do it. When you seek revenge, you are making the battle yours and not trusting God to fight your battles for you. God's victories and justice always eclipse any of the outcomes you could hope to achieve in your limited human power.

Here is a practical example of "how" and "what" to pray for someone who is at odds with you; *"Lord, I pray for NAME that he or she will be happy, healthy, prosperous, content, blessed, loved, and receive good things in their life."* Again, this is really hard to do in the natural. Psychologically, it is harder to hate someone when you are praying blessings for them rather than curses. It helps to understand that in God's spiritual law "like energies attract like energies." This is the principle behind *sowing and reaping*. What you send out into the universe [good or bad] will begin to manifest in your life over time.

Everything is energy in vibration [at different frequencies]. Love has a much higher vibrational frequency than hate or revenge. It is often said there is "POWER in the spoken word." This is true in spiritual law. What you think, say and do is what you vibrate to. Again in spiritual law, like energies attract like energies. Choose to vibrate [your mind and body] to only good, positive, happy and loving things and that is what you will attract back into your life.

Know that the same is true of anger, hate and revenge. God gives you free will and you get to choose what you vibrate to and attract into your life. Scripture says in Proverbs 18:21 the power of life and death is in the power of the tongue [your spoken word] and those who indulge in it will eat the fruit of it. So choose life rather than death. Love > hate.

Know that spiritual law trumps physical law. When you pray to bless someone, you are putting positive good energies into the universe and you will begin to attract positive good things back into your life. What you think, say and do consistently will begin to shape your life. The positive energies you *sow* cause physical molecules to begin to realign and will manifest in your life and circumstances as you *reap* your harvest.

Turning the other cheek is the physical way to put the spiritual law of "non-resistance" into motion. When you remain undisturbed by an adverse situation, it will fall away of its own weight. When you have no emotional response to an inharmonious situation, it will fade away from your pathway. Conversely, when you respond to situations and linger in anger, hate or revenge, you will attract even more of that inharmonious situation [or person] back into your life. You can run but you cannot hide until you forgive and become undisturbed [non-resistant] to the person who is your adversary.

The great robbers of time, peace and contentment are the past and the future. You should bless the past and then forget it or it will keep you in bondage. Bless the future [trusting God] with expectations of many happy surprises, but do not obsess [worry] about it. What you are to do is to live fully in the NOW trusting God's love to provide your provision and protection. Also, trust in God's justice to bring about the right things sooner or later in His perfect timing and in His perfect way. Set aside all anger and thoughts of revenge so you can fully receive and experience God's blessing in your life "NOW."

There is a high spiritual price to pay when you take revenge. You will *reap what you sow,* so don't sow revenge unless you are prepared to accept [reap] the negative consequences.

Know that our God is a god of both love and justice. Walk in His love and trust in His justice. When you do this, know that you will be repaid by God in multiples [double] for the injustices others have done to you. See Job 42:10 and Isaiah 61:7. We serve a God of double portion. Be assured that God's word will come to pass in your life and He will restore double to you.

My obedience level to this command is:

12. Be perfect (walk Holy before our Holy God, be sinless)

Matthew 5:48 *"You, therefore will be perfect* [growing into spiritual maturity both in mind and character, actively integrating Godly values into your daily life], *as your heavenly Father is perfect."*

Leviticus 19:2 '… you shall be holy for I the Lord your God am holy.'

Commentary on What to Know and Do:

Strive to be perfect as your Father in Heaven is perfect. Proactively try to eliminate all conscious sin from your life and walk holy before our holy God. Aspire to live with the same kind of generosity and graciousness God directs toward you, His creation. Know that "holy" means to be 'special, consecrated, and set apart to be used by God for His purposes.' Just as Jesus was holy, we too are to be holy to carry on His ministry on earth.

As human beings, we know that we will never be perfect, but we should make a serious effort to be more Christ-like each day. This involves knowing His words and teachings and then obeying them to the best of our ability. Ask the Holy Spirit (the Helper) for help in this area of your life.

My obedience level to this command is:

13. Practice secret disciplines (giving, praying, fasting)

Matthew 6:1-8 *"Be [very] careful not to do your good deeds publicly, to be seen by men, otherwise you will have no reward [prepared and awaiting you] with your Father who is in heaven."*

"So whenever you give to the poor and do acts of kindness, do not blow a trumpet before you [to advertise it] as the hypocrites do [like actors acting out a role] in the synagogues and in the streets, so that they can be honored and recognized and praised by men. I assure you and most solemnly say to you, they [already] have their reward in full."

"but when you give to the poor and do acts of kindness, do not let your left hand know what your right hand is doing [give in complete secrecy], so that your charitable acts will be done in secret, and your Father sees [what is done] in secret will reward you."

"also when you pray, do not be like the hypocrites; for they love to pray [publicly] standing in the synagogues and on the corners of the streets so that they may be seen by men. I assure you and most solemnly say to you, they [already] have their reward in full."

'But when you pray, go into your most private room, close the door and pray to the father who is in secret, and your father who sees [what is done] in secret will reward you."

"and when you pray, do not use meaningless repetition as the Gentile do, for they think they will be heard because of their many words. So do not be like them [praying as they do]; for your Father knows what you need before you ask Him."

Commentary on What to Know and Do:

Don't show off your generosity. When you give to others don't make a fuss over it. Do your good deeds in private. God always knows what you did and he values your unselfish heart attitude (motive). Strive to please God, not men. Know that there are rewards in heaven for your humility and generosity.

Make time each day to retreat to your private place and pray [talk with] the Lord. Do this in private and not in public for show. Be generous in private with your gifts to worthy causes and charities. Do it unselfishly with the heart attitude [motives] of blessing other people rather than selfishly accumulating social capital for yourself. Give generously and privately expecting nothing in return in this life. Know that your rewards will be great in the next life. Again, you will *"reap what you sow."*

My obedience level to this command is:

14. Lay up treasures in Heaven

Matthew 6:19-21   *"Do not store up for yourselves* [material] *treasures on earth, where moth and rust destroy, and where thieves break in and steal. But store up for yourselves treasures in heaven, where neither moth nor rust destroys, and where thieves do not break in and steal; for where your treasure is, there your heart* [your wishes, your desires; that on which your life centers] *will be also."*

Luke 6:38   *"Give, and it will be given to you. They will pour into your lap a good measure-pressed down, shaken together, and running over* [with no space left for more]. *For with the standard of measurement you use* [when you do good to others], *it will be measured to you in return."*

Luke 16:10-12   *"He who is faithful in a very little thing is also faithful in much; and he who is dishonest in a very little thing is also dishonest in much. Therefore, if you have not been faithful in the use of earthly wealth, who will entrust the true riches to you? And if you have not been faithful in the use of that [earthly wealth] which belongs to another [whether God or man, and of which you are a trustee], who will give you that which is not your own?"*

Commentary on What to Know and Do:

Invest in things that matter eternally, like the welfare of other people. Know that the acquisition of earthly wealth and possessions is "short-sighted" and temporary. Seek to deploy your time, energies and resources in advancing the Kingdom of God as the Holy Spirit directs you daily. Praise God regularly and be a blessing to as many people as you can every day.

Keep in mind that in the spiritual law of *giving and receiving [sowing and reaping]* "helping is healing." When you take your eyes off yourself to help someone in greater need, the Lord will begin to supernaturally meet your needs and heal your issues.

Know that money is God's favorite way to test you. God often tests you first to see if you are responsible with your finances and material possessions before He will trust you with spiritual power. God's blessing are not automatically given to everybody and anybody. He is looking at your heart attitude, your actions and your obedience to His commands, especially with money. How you use your money shows what you love the most. Wherever you want your heart to be, put your time, energy and money into it. God loves [and blesses] a cheerful giver versus one who gives out of reluctance or a sense of obligation. God often tests us in small things before He gives us bigger things and spiritual power to bless us and others.

It is a cliched analogy that says: "If you were on trial for being a Christian, would there be enough evidence in your checkbook, your credit card statements and your calendar to convict you?"

Money is the acid test of your faith in God and His promises, but it also shows God He can trust you. Are you a trustworthy steward in your use of the treasures God provides you?

My obedience level to this command is:

15. Seek first the kingdom of God

Matthew 6:33 *"But first and most importantly seek* [aim at, strive after] *His kingdom and His righteousness* [His way of doing and being right - the attitude and character of God], *and all these things will be given to you."*

Commentary on What to Know and Do:

Seek first a personal relationship with God and then trust Him to provide for your needs because He loves you. Know that you, as a believer, are adopted into His family and, as an heir, you are entitled to God's benefits. (described well in Ps 103) Do not be consumed with worry about what you will eat, drink or wear. Know that God is your provider. Keep God first place in your life. If Jesus' words abide in you and you abide (stay, dwell, rest, relax) in them, all things you need will be provided.

This command tells us to seek after His righteousness. We do this when we seek to purge sin(s) from our lives and love others as Jesus loves us. Try hard to always be in "right-standing" with God, the Father. Do everything for the Glory of the Father and to advance His kingdom on earth.

The Kingdom is the realm of right [perfect] ideas which includes God's divine pattern and purpose for you. There is a place that you are to fill; no one else can fill it. There is something you are to do that no one else can do. Always seek God's will for your life and pray for His divine blessings intended specifically for you. When you do this, God will bring you every righteous desire of your heart including love, peace, joy, contentment, health, friends, prosperity, perfect self-expression and His highest ideals for your life. Know that if and when you strive for things that do not belong to you by divine right [contrary to God's divine plan for you] you will obtain only frustration, failure, dissatisfaction and you may not be able to keep [retain] it for long.

Realize that God is your supply and you can release all that belongs to you by divine right through your spoken word. You must have perfect faith in your spoken word and then act in perfect faith. You are instructed in Romans 4:17 to call forth things [within the will of God] that are not [yet] manifested and you will have them. You must act in perfect faith in preparation to receive your God-given blessings as described in 2 Kings 3:6 [dig ditches in the desert preparing to receive the requested rain from God]. God is your supply and there is a supply for every righteous demand [prayer request].

Rather than be anxious or worry, Jesus tells you how to better use the energies you might have invested [wasted] in worry. He says that if you seek God's Kingdom first, everything you need will be provided for you. God already knows your needs and His will is to provide for you. Before you call, He has answers on your path. Pray that God's will be done on earth [in and through your life] as it is in heaven. This is seeking first the Kingdom of God and His righteousness.

My obedience level to this command is:

16. Don't judge others (judge not)

Matthew 7:1-2 *"DO NOT judge and criticize and condemn [others unfairly with an attitude of self-righteous superiority as though assuming the office of a judge], so that you will not be judged* [unfairly]. *For just as you* [hypocritically] *judge others* [when you are sinful and unrepentant], *so will you be judged; and in accordance with your standard of measure* [used to pass out judgment], *judgment will be measured to you."*

Commentary on What to Know and Do:

Know that it is God's role to judge people and not your role. Also know that if you judge others, God will judge you by the same standards you have applied. Work hard to resist the temptation to judge other people. If you are judgmental, you will be judged [by God]. This is part of the spiritual law of "like energies attract like energies" which is the spiritual basis of *sowing and reaping* in the Bible. When you send out judgement, you will get judgement in return. Many religions of the world refer to this spiritual principle as Karma, although that term is not used in the Christian Bible. Judgement creates a Karmic debt [sin debt] that demands repayment.

Judgement opens a door to the enemy [Satan]. This is why you need to learn not to be critical or judgmental of others. In related scripture [Matthew 7:4-5], Jesus tells us to focus less on what may be wrong with others and focus more on what is wrong with us [and fix it].

Sadly, many Christians have earned a reputation for being judgmental, which is just the opposite of what Jesus commanded. When you judge from a "holier than thou" basis, you are walking in a spirit of pride and not humility. A good quote from Joyce Meyer says *"Anywhere you do not have a responsibility, it's smart not to offer an opinion."*

Have you ever wondered what the difference is in having an opinion versus being judgmental? The topic of abortion provides a good [and controversial] example. You could have the opinion and belief that abortion is the *"shedding of innocent blood"* for the sake of convenience. You become judgmental when you start focusing on what you believe the fate will be for the person performing the abortion or for the person receiving the abortion. It is God's role to judge and determine the eternal fate of any individual, and not yours. Judging usually involves dwelling on something negative over and over in your mind.

Know that "judging others" is a sin into which many of us easily fall. It is one of those traps of Satan that is pretty effective. When you find yourself dwelling on something negative about someone, be quick to realize it is the sin of judgement. Remember that judging others is God's job and not yours. Repent quickly of your sin of judgment and turn it over to God to do His job. He is the God of both love and justice and He will work it out in His own sovereign way.

My obedience level to this command is:

17. Do not throw your pearls to pigs

Matthew 7:6 *"Do not give that which is holy to dogs, and do not throw your pearles before pigs, for they will trample them under their feet, and turn and tear you to pieces."*

Commentary on What to Know and Do:

Do not persist in sharing your faith and the Gospel with people who do not wish to hear it. If you determine your message is unwelcomed and totally rejected, be comfortable in just politely walking away. Do your best to be Jesus' ambassador and then trust God for the rest. It is the Holy spirit's job to convict their heart, not yours. Trust God to do what you cannot do and then be at peace about it.

In Matthew 7:6, Jesus actually commanded His disciples not to share their faith with people who did not want to hear it. That same command still applies to us today. Remember, not everyone is called by God to be *His sheep*.

My obedience level to this command is:

18. Ask, seek, knock

Matthew 7:7-8   *"Ask and keep on asking and it will be given to you, seek and keep on seeking and you will find; knock and keep on knocking and the door will be opened to you. [Luke 11:9-13]. For everyone who keeps on asking receives, and he who keeps on seeking finds, and to him who keeps on knocking, it will be opened."*

<u>Commentary on What to Know and Do:</u>

When you pray, ask God for wisdom and to meet your daily needs. Trust Him to be your provider and protector. Realize He will do this because He loves you and has adopted you as a Believer into His family. When you ask, seek, and knock, it honors and pleases God because you surrender and acknowledge your dependence on Him. Come to Him diligently. Remember that Jesus loves to answer your prayers and to give you what you seek so that your joy may be made full and the Father is glorified.

Jesus invites us to come freely to God and present our requests to Him. Come boldly, be direct and ask for what you need. Jesus clearly states that you will receive, find, and the doors will be opened to you. Jesus responds to those who seek Him diligently, not casually.

My obedience level to this command is:

THE 50 COMMANDS OF JESUS

19. Treat others as you would like to be treated (do unto others)

Matthew 7:12   *"So then, in everything treat others the same way you want them to treat you, for this is [the essence of] of the Law and the [writings of the] Prophets."*

Commentary on What to Know and Do:

   Treat others in the same good manner you would like to be treated. This is commonly called the Golden Rule. This is one of the most famous commands of Christ Jesus. Know that when you think, say and do good deeds to bless others, you are putting the principles of love and sowing and reaping into action. In spiritual law "like energies attract like energies," you will attract similar good things back into your life.
   This would be a much better world if all people would put this command into practice. Sadly, too many people let pride, greed and selfishness get in their way. Do your best to love people and treat them the same good way you would like to be treated whether they reciprocate or not. Know that your rewards will come in Heaven. There is an old Jewish belief that for every good deed you do, it adds a pearl to your crown in Heaven. Go through life being obedient to Jesus by treating others well and adding to your Heavenly crown.

   My obedience level to this command is:

20. Choose the narrow way

Matthew 7:13-14   *"Enter through the narrow gate. For wide is the gate and broad and easy to travel is the path that leads to destruction and eternal loss, and there are many who enter through it. But small is the gate and narrow and difficult to travel is the path that leads the way to* [everlasting] *life, and there are few who find it."*

Commentary on What to Know and Do:

Know that there are two different interpretations of this command. The common interpretation says there are two paths/gates: one leads to Heaven and the other leads to Hell [the two destinies that await the human race]. The path to Heaven is narrow and difficult, not many people will choose this gate. Only a few will find it and go in; those few who believe in and follow Jesus in faith calling Him Lord and obey His commands. The path to Hell is broad and easy and it attracts many people to it. Those who choose this route are bound for destruction and Hell because they have rejected Jesus and choose not to believe He is the only path to salvation.

A less common interpretation applies only to Christians. There is a spiritual gateway and a carnal gateway. The spiritual path leads to abundant and victorious life, and the carnal path results in the loss of reward for a wasted and defeated life. The spiritual path requires true disciples to have discipline, dedication, and death to self while producing *good fruit*. The carnal path results in a life without meaning; a wasted life where Christ was not central and God was not glorified. Such a life does not produce *good fruit*.

Know that the way to God and eternal life is clearly spelled out in scripture: faith and belief in our heart confessed with our mouth that Jesus is the Christ, and that he was crucified and resurrected as atonement for our sins. Know that your salvation is faith-based and not works-based. There are no shortcuts to that eternal life with God, so don't look for any. The world is full of self-help tips for a successful life here on earth. Many in the crowd live carnally-minded and only for today's pleasures with little thought about being within the will of God for their lives. This is not the path leading to the "narrow gate." Don't just follow the herd through the wide gate but seek the narrow gate that leads to God and eternal life. Obedience to Jesus' words and commands place us within the *will of God* and help us along the path leading to the "narrow gate."

My obedience level to this command is:

21. Beware of false prophets

Matthew 7:15   *"Beware of the false prophets* [teachers]*who come to you dressed as sheep* [appearing gentle and innocent] *but inwardly are ravenous wolves."*

Commentary on What to Know and Do:

Look for and do not be fooled by a "wolf in sheep's clothing." This can apply to those who claim to be religious leaders, prophets, and make false religious claims. They are deceptive and dangerous. A religious leader may appear to be wise and respectable, but you must look at the fruits of his life to know if he truly represents God and does the will of the Father.

Be cautious of a preacher with great charisma, but is shallow in character. Look carefully to see if he produces *good fruit, no fruit, or bad fruit* in his ministry. There are many false teachers who have practiced smiles and drip with honey and practiced sincerity before their audiences. Make sure they are not trying to rip you off in one way or another. A genuine leader who is a man [or woman] of God will not try to exploit your pocketbook or your emotions. Know that some people start out with sincere hearts for God but become corrupted by power, fame, greed, money, etc. over time. Good discernment is required on your part to determine if the preacher is a person of good character whose life produces *good fruit* and whose messages align fully with God's word - the Bible. If not, beware.

My obedience level to this command is:

22. Pray for more helpers

Matthew 9:37-38 *"Then He said to His disciples, 'The harvest is [indeed] plentiful, but the workers are few. So pray to the Lord of the harvest to send out workers into His harvest."*

Commentary on What to Know and Do:

Pray to the Lord who is in charge of the harvest and ask Him to send more workers into His fields. Jesus saw many people who were ready to believe in Him but realized there were too few workers to go out to the masses ready to be harvested. Jesus asks His followers today to participate in the solution to this problem. We are to pray and send out helpers [missionaries and evangelists], or to go ourselves.

God's will is to bless people [His creation]. He wants to do many good things for His people [*His sheep*], but there are not enough people [*believers*] who are willing to spend much of their time for the betterment of their fellow man. Jesus commands us to pray for more people to help in bringing the Kingdom of Heaven to earth.

My obedience level to this command is:

23. Be wise and inoffensive

Matthew 10:16   *"Listen carefully, I am sending you out like sheep among wolves; so be wise as serpents, and innocent as doves* [have no self-serving agendas]."

Romans 6:19   ... *offer your members* [abilities and talents] *as slaves to righteousness, leading to sanctification* [that is being set apart for God's purposes].

Commentary on What to Know and Do:

Jesus empowered His disciples and gave them specific instructions to preach, heal the sick, cast out demons and to proclaim the Kingdom of God. He told them to take care because He was sending them into a world ruled by Satan.

Like the original disciples, you are to be wise as to what is good and innocent versus what is evil. Today, you are to preach, heal, and proclaim the Gospel as you also apply wisdom concerning the evil world into which you are sent. Offer your talents and abilities for God's purposes to advance the Kingdom of God as you walk in righteousness.

Jesus commands you to be wise and innocent of self-serving motives as you share your faith and the Gospel with others. Know that many will not be open or receptive to hearing about the Gospel. Nevertheless, go out boldly, but practice wisdom, humility and innocence as Christ's ambassador on earth.

My obedience level to this command is:

24. Fear God, do not fear man

Matthew 10:28 *"Do not be afraid of those who kill the body, but cannot kill the soul; but rather be afraid of Him who can destroy both the soul and the body in hell."*

Luke 12:4-5 *"I say to you, My Friends, do not be afraid of those who kill the body and after that they have nothing more they can do to you. But I will point out to you whom you should fear; fear the One who, after He has killed, has the authority and power to hurl you into hell; yes, I say to you,* [stand in great awe of God and] *fear Him."*

Commentary on What to Know and Do:

Do not fear man who can only kill your body but not your soul. Instead fear [reverence, great and profound respect] God who can both kill your body and condemn your soul to Hell. Know that the death of the body is not the ultimate loss, but the deaths of the body and the soul together in Hell are the ultimate loss. Physical death is simply a doorway to your resurrected life in Heaven [for a believer in Christ Jesus].

Life is fragile and fleeting, so there is a need to be "prayed up" at all times. As the country western song by Kenny Chesney says, *"Everybody wants to go to heaven; but nobody wants to go now"* and the lyrics from Lorretta Lynn say *"Everybody want to go to heaven, but nobody wants to die Lord."* Even though God gives you free will to make many choices in life, you do not get to choose the how or the when of your death, unless you decide to commit suicide.

Note: This author believes that a person who commits suicide condemns themself to Hell. Suicide is a permanent solution to what are usually temporary problems. It is the sin of murder [murder of self]. There are some seriously negative consequences for choosing this route. Don't risk losing your resurrected life with your eternity in Heaven with Lord Jesus and Abba Father. Don't cause hurt and pain in those who do care about you.

THE 50 COMMANDS OF JESUS

Don't allow bullies to coerce you into silence. Know that your spirit is your core being, and there is nothing any man [human] can do to your spirit man. Save your fear [reverence] for God who holds your entire life [body, soul and spirit] in His hands and trust that He will be with you to the end of times.

My obedience level to this command is:

25. Listen to God's voice

Matthew 11:15, 13:9   *"He who has ears to hear, let him hear and heed My words."*

Matthew 13:43   *"then THE RIGHTEOUS [those who seek the will of God] WILL SHINE FORTH [radiating the new life] LIKE THE SUN in the kingdom of their Father. He who has ears [to hear] let him hear and heed my words."*

Mark 4:23   *"If anyone has ears to hear, let him hear and heed My words."*

Luke 14:35   *"It [tasteless salt] is fit neither for the soil nor for the manure pile; it is thrown away. He who has ears to hear, let him hear and heed My words."*

Commentary on What to Know and Do:

When God speaks something important to you, you are to listen carefully. "He who has ears, let him hear." Some teachings [like the parables] require you to listen carefully and interpret them with more than just ordinary powers of speech and words. You are to give the highest attention to what was spoken by Jesus, take it in deeply and remember it. Know that part of the role of the Holy Spirit is to be a teacher who will bring to you the remembrance [top-of-mind] of Jesus' teachings when you need them. This assumes you already have them deep within your heart from previous study of God's Word.

Take heed of what you hear. The more you hear, the more will be shared. Do not let your ears become hard of hearing and your heart grow hard to God's voice. Know that God often speaks to you clearly through His Word [the Bible] and that "still small voice." It is vitally important that you not only hear but also [heed] obey what you are told to do. Many times God's directions do not make sense in the natural, but you are to step out in faith and obey. There is an old saying which says "if it doesn't make sense in the natural, it is probably from God."

Many times God will only reveal one step at a time to you. He often waits on your obedience before revealing the next step(s) in your journey. We humans often want to see the whole route and know the final destination before we even start moving. Know that God frequently does not reveal every step at one time, but He does reveal your final destination of Heaven [if you are a born again Believer in Christ Jesus].

Take time to carefully consider what God is saying to you and determine "what" you are to do. You will not always know the "why," but be obedient to hear the "what" and then do it. When you pray [to God], do not forget to listen and obey. Pray-Listen-Obey.

My obedience level to this command is:

26. Cast your burdens onto Him [take my yoke]

Matthew 11:28-30   *"Come to Me, all who are weary and heavy burdened* [by religious rituals that provide no peace]*, and I will give you rest* [refreshing your souls with salvation]*. Take My yoke upon you and learn from me* [following Me as My disciple] *for I am gentle* *and humble in heart, and YOU WILL FIND REST* [renewal, blessed quiet] *FOR YOUR SOULS. For My yoke is easy* [to bear] *and My burden is light."*

Commentary on What to Know and Do:

Know that when you choose to become "yoked" with Jesus, He will guide and direct your life in ways that make your life easier and bring peace and rest to your soul [mind]. Jesus instructs you to lay down your burdens and rest in Him. His yoke is easy to bear and His burden is light.

His commandments are not burdensome but rather guide you into God's will for your life and blessings begin to flow. Going God's way brings rest to your soul; going your own way in life will never bring rest. Let the God of peace have full control over your life. Be happy to be "yoked" to Jesus and allow Him to carry your load. Let go and let God [Jesus] carry your burdens in life.

Let God fight your battles for you. This requires faith and trust that God loves you and wants to bless, protect, and provide for you as a member of His adopted family. You are to surrender both your strengths and weaknesses to the Lord and allow Him to carry your load and fight your battles. God's victories in your life will always be greater than what you could ever hope to achieve in your own limited human power.

Imagine for a moment a huge steel beam weighing many tons. On earth, it is the physical law of gravity [in our three-dimensional physical world] that gives that beam its weight. If that beam was to be suddenly transported into outer space [in a fourth dimension away from all physical gravity] it would have no weight. This analogy illustrates that the spiritual realm functions very differently in the supernatural fourth dimension as compared to the physical realm of the three-dimensional Earth that we humans live in.

Know that the Trinity [God, Jesus and the Holy Spirit] function in the supernatural fourth dimension realm of spiritual law. God created man as a three-part being: body, soul and spirit. Your soul is the energy of your brain with its memory, will, and emotion. The energy of your mind is where heaven and earth intersect [the spiritual and the physical realms]. Part of your free will is to make choices and decisions. When you consciously [mentally] choose to cast your burdens on Christ Jesus, you are directing your vibratory energy into the spiritual realm of God, that fourth dimension. That fourth-dimensional spiritual realm where Jesus is the master [of spiritual law] and all things are possible. Know that spiritual law of God trumps physical law here on earth. He [Jesus] is able to bring you supernatural peace and reduce the weight of your earthly burdens. In the spiritual realm of God there is only perfection, completion, joy and life. Active faith serves as the bridge for God's blessings to flow supernaturally from the spiritual realm to manifest in your physical life and circumstances.

At times you may pray to go completely around your problems [burdens], but more often than not Jesus gives you the strength and peace to go through them if you ask and trust Him to do so. He tells [commands] you to do this. Be obedient to His command and choose to cast your burdens on Him. Fear and worry are misdirected energies that need to be redirected into faith in Jesus and his promise in John 10:10 to *bring you abundant life, to the full and overflowing.* Know that fear and worry are a form of disobedience, so don't go there.

Stand still in faith [remain calm, poised and patient] and let the Lord fight your battles supernaturally. Cast your burdens on the Lord and then depend on His strength and not yours. Psalm 55 tells you to "cast thy burden upon the Lord." One practical way to do this is to make this powerful declarative statement:

"I now cast my burden(s) of _____ on the Christ within [the Holy Spirit], and I go free to enjoy peace and _____." (Fill in the blanks for your specific needs and circumstances.)

This powerful statement should be **spoken out loud** over and over with faith and no doubt. Its effect will be to wind you up with the power of the spoken word. Know that the power of your spoken word is amplified [multiplied] when it is aligned with God's will and the Word of God. Don't carry the weights [burdens] Christ Jesus never intended for you to carry. That is His job if you let Him.

My obedience level to this command is:

27. Honor your parents

Matthew 15:4 *"For God said* [through Moses], *"HONOR YOUR FATHER AND MOTHER', and 'HE WHO SPEAKS EVIL OF, or INSULTS or TREATS IMPROPERLY FATHER OR MOTHER IS TO BE PUT TO DEATH!"* [Ex 20:12, 21:17; Liv20:9, Duet 5:16]

Matthew 15:5-7 *But you say, 'If anyone says to his father and mother, "Whatever* [money or resources that] *I have that would help you is* [already dedicated and] *given to God* [the temple] (due to the selfish and inappropriate practice of CORBAN) *he is not honoring his father or mother* [by helping them with their need]. *"So by this you have invalidated the word of God for the sake of your traditions* [handed down by the elders]. *You hypocrites…"*

Commentary on What to Know and Do:

Know that Jesus was especially critical of the hypocrisy of the Pharisees [religious leaders]. One example that Jesus was highly critical of was the misuse [by the Pharisees and temple authorities] of the practice of **Corban**. Corban was an offering dedicated to the temple that could not be used for any other purpose.

The commandment to honor your parents has often been interpreted to mean that children must care for elderly parents and even support them if they slip into ill health and/or poverty. This support for one's parents is a commandment of God and should be observed faithfully, both then and now.

The religious leaders in Jesus' day condoned the use of Corban so people would pledge financial support to the temple while avoiding their God-given commandment to support [honor] their parents. The religious leaders of the temple were focused more on what they could selfishly obtain for their use in the temple rather than obeying God's command to honor [care for] parents. This was just one of the many hypocrisies Jesus railed against by the religious leaders of His day. They enforced their many man-made laws while completely missing God altogether.

Honor, respect and obey your parents. If you curse them, disrespect them, or fail to care for them, there may be bad and negative consequences in your life, both in the natural and in the spiritual. Know that Scripture says anyone speaking evil of their parent must end in death [probably spiritual death].

Contemporary Western society and law do not permit a parent killing a child for disrespect, but this author believes there are spiritual consequences for disrespecting and failing to honor and care for parents. Such disrespect is a sin [disobedience to a command of Jesus] and can lead to generational curses passed down to the 3rd and 4th generations. The good news is that generational curses can be broken by specific prayer.

Sadly, in today's society, young people have little respect for the authority of their parents or grandparents [or anyone else like teachers, police, etc.]. The formula for modern TV sitcoms presents a family with children regularly talking back [disrespecting] to parents. That TV formula for humor often presents the father as a buffoon who is not honored or respected by either his wife or children. In today's many broken homes, the father may not even be present, much less honored or respected.

Know that honor, trust, and respect are hard to earn and easy to lose. Parents must do their part to be worthy of that honor, trust and respect from their children even though society pulls the children in a different direction. This pull to destroy the family is one of the many tactics of the evil one. Just be sure you are obedient to honor your parents and set a good example for your children [whether or not it is returned to you by your children].

Teach your children from a very young age to honor their parents and grandparents. Their words and behaviors need to demonstrate that respect and honor. Studies of learning and child development conclude that if good practices are not ingrained in a child by the age of 10, it may be too late. Obviously, with God all things are possible [no matter the age]. Too many parents today are not diligent in teaching or requiring children to show respect.

One of the key differences in parenting today, versus 50 years ago, is that the wants and desires of the children come first today. Fifty years ago the wants and needs of the parents, grandparents, and family came first. In real life, priorities must flex and change from moment to moment, but in general parents today have consistently given first place to the wants and whims of the children. The consequence of this is a generation of spoiled, self-centered, and "entitled" young people who have little concern for what's best for the family. They have not been taught respect and honor. It remains to be seen if they will "honor their parents" in the long run down the road.

While Corban is not a practice of most Christians today, you are commanded to honor and care for your parents in both the 10 Commandments of Moses and by the commands of Christ Jesus.

My obedience level to this command is:

28. Beware of false teaching

Matthew 16:6, 11-12   Jesus said to them, *Watch out and be on your guard against the leven [yeast] of the Pharisees and Sadducees. How is it that you fail to understand that I was not talking to you about bread? But beware of the leven [false teachings] of the Pharisees and Sadducees.*

Commentary on What to Know and Do:

Beware of the leven [yeast] of the Pharisees. Know that yeast was often a metaphor for evil in Jewish teaching. Be on guard for teachers who teach false doctrines and ideas. Following those wrong ideas can lead to enormously wrong beliefs. Test and compare all teaching you hear against the Word of God, the Bible. Beware if there is little or no alignment. Also, beware if there is little or no *good fruit* produced by their lives, teachings and ministries.

Know that Satan can often appear as an angel of light [2 Corinthians 11:14]. He and his demonic forces can and do change their skin and appearance to deceive believers. It is important for believers to study and know the Word of God, the Bible. Without this foundation of God's truths in your life you can be an easy target of Satan's deceptions and lies. Remember that Satan's goal is to keep you away from God and to steal, kill and destroy your life [John 10:10]. Satan often uses the leven [evil] of false teachers as one of his many deceptive ploys.

At the time of Jesus' life and 3.5 year ministry, the religious system of the day was based primarily on rule-keeping as the means of obtaining salvation. Jesus was very critical of the religious leaders who were the gatekeepers of this performance-based system. He often called them out as hypocrites. When He announced that He was the Messiah spoken of in scripture by the prophets of old, His claims and criticisms ultimately angered the religious leaders to the point they demand His death. Jesus told them they were hypocrites and that their many man-made rules completely missed God.

From these lessons, you are to beware of performance-based religion and the many false teachers out there.

My obedience level to this command is:

29. Deny yourself

Luke 9:23   And He was saying to them all, *"If anyone wishes to follow Me* [as My disciple], *he must deny himself* [set aside selfish interests], *and take up his cross daily* [expressing a willingness to endure whatever may come], *and follow Me* [believing in Me, conforming to My example in living and, if need be, suffering or perhaps dying because of faith in Me.]"

Matthew 10:38   *"And he who does not take his cross* [expressing a willingness to endure whatever may come] *and follow Me is not worthy of Me."*

Mark 8:34   Jesus called the crowd together with His disciples, and said to them, *"If anyone wishes to follow Me* [as my disciple] *he must deny himself* [set aside selfish interests], *and take up his cross* [conforming to My example in living]."

Commentary on What to Know and Do:

    Choose to love Jesus more than anyone else (including family) and live for Him alone. Be willing to let go of your own personal agendas, desires, wishes, dreams and ways of living to walk the difficult path of Christ fully submitted to the will of God for you and your life. Know that those who follow Jesus will find the life that is true and those who go their own way will lose their lives, no matter what they find on earth. Be so willing to deny yourself that you are willing to follow and die for your faith in Christ.

    Those who follow Jesus should be willing to say daily "Not my will, but your will be done" today on earth as it is in heaven. A good practical way to follow Jesus in living the will of God is to ask the Holy Spirit in your morning prayer to show you what God is doing in your sphere of influence and what your role is in it. Too many times we ask God to bless our plans rather than we earnestly seek to bless and act on God's plan. Figuratively, like in a play, we want to read from our own script when we should be reading from God's script.

    If you look honestly at how you spend your time and thought energy, you can determine who or what truly "sits on the throne of your life." This simple self-analysis shows the location [focus] your heart. Your focus should be on Jesus more than anything else like sports, the pursuit of money, material possessions, family, job, career, success, sex, working out, hobbies, travel, etc..

Jesus said multiple times that if we love Him and want to follow Him we should know his teachings and obey his commands. That still applies to you and me today.

My obedience level to this command is:

30. Do not despise little ones

Matthew 18:10   *"See that you do not despise or think less of these little ones. For I say to you that their angels in heaven* [are in the presence of and] *continually look upon the face of My Father who is in heaven."*

Commentary on What to Know and Do:

Be kind to little children. Jesus commands us not to look down on little children, but to welcome them. See that you do not look down on, hinder, despise, or think less of any young people who are trying to make their way to Jesus . Know that their angels in heaven are looking after them as they seek to see the face of the Father who is in Heaven.

Jesus disciples tried to keep the little children away from Him because they thought He was too busy and important to spend time with children. He rebuked them for this and said to let the children come to Him. Just as Jesus welcomed the children, he welcomes any of us who seek Him. We are all God's children and he loves us unconditionally.

Know that the "little ones" can apply to more than just children. It can also apply to a new believer who is not yet mature and/or strong in their faith. You are to help them grow in their knowledge and spiritual maturity. You should not be "puffed up" because you are further along in your spiritual walk than someone else.

My obedience level to this command is:

31. Go directly to Christians who offend you

Matthew 18:15   *"If your brother sins, go and show him his fault in private; if he listens and pays attention to you, you have won back your brother."*

Galatians 6:1   BROTHERS, If anyone is caught in any sin, you who are spiritual [you who are responsive to the guidance of the Spirit] are to restore such a person in a spirit of gentleness [not with a sense of superiority or self-righteousness], keeping a watchful eye on yourself, so that you are not tempted as well.

Commentary on What to Know and Do:

If a fellow Christian brother wrongs you by either his words or actions, you should not complain of it to others. Instead, you should go directly to him in private to state the matter kindly, show him [describe] his conduct and explain its negative impact. Press it home in such a way to reach his reason and consciousness. If he listens to you, you have won a brother. Know that a little friendly conversation can often set the matter straight and avoid further difficulty.

Today, too few people take this commanded direct approach. Many people would welcome the opportunity of acknowledging their wrong conduct and make it right. It is your obligation to furnish them the opportunity. Remember that angry words spoken in front of others often fail to reach the desired outcome. In life it is best to "praise publicly and criticize privately."

Galatians 6:1 reminds us to approach a person [who has sinned and needs correction] with gentleness and avoid having a spirit of superiority or self-righteousness. Know that when you attempt to correct or counsel family members [especially teens and adults], it is often very difficult and fails miserably. What constructive counsel [advice] you provide with good intentions and with a loving heart is often received as judgement and/or criticism by family members. Try your best, but also pray that the Holy Spirit brings someone into their life with a similar message they will receive. Keep this old adage in mind: Rules without relationship lead to rebellion.

Jesus commands you and me to try our best to be constructive in restoring broken relationships.

My obedience level to this command is:

32. Forgive offenders

Matthew 6:12   *"And forgive us our debts, as we have forgiven our debtors* [letting go of both the wrong and the resentment].

Matthew 6:14-15   *"For if you forgive others their trespasses* [their reckless and willful sins] *your heavenly Father will also forgive you. But if you do not forgive others* [nurturing your hurt and anger with the result that it interferes with your relationship with God], *then your Father will not forgive your trespasses."*

Matthew 18-21   Then Peter came to Him and asked, *"Lord, how many times will my brother sin against me and I forgive him and let it go? Up to seven times?"*

Jesus answered him and said, *"I say to you, not up to seven times, but seventy times seven."*

Proverbs 19:11   Good sense and discretion make a man slow to anger, and it is his honor and glory to overlook a transgression or offense [without seeking revenge and harboring resentment].

Commentary on What to Know and Do:

We are commanded to forgive people who offend us or do us wrong an unlimited number of times. It often takes wisdom, patience and obedience to overlook the offences of others. Sometimes this is described as "non-resistance" in spiritual law. Know that we will not be forgiven of our offenses (sins) unless we forgive others. Peter asked Jesus about forgiving someone 7 times in a day, and Jesus told him 70 X 7, which really means an unlimited number of times.

Highly important spiritual concepts are usually repeated in many places in the Bible. To "forgive" or "forgiveness" shows up many times depending on which translation you are studying at. Approximately one-third of those mentions are tied to forgiving others. Forgiveness is not optional; it is a command. Number of mentions in various translations:

KJV - 95
ESV - 109
NIV - 81
Contemporary English Version - 206

Know that there are negative consequences to unforgiveness. When you are constantly angry and walk in constant unforgiveness, you open spiritual and physical doorways for problems, sickness and disease to manifest in your life. Modern medicine confirms in many studies that anger, hate and bitterness lead to health problems. Unforgiving people are usually unhappy people.

Speak forgiveness out loud and do it quickly through an act of obedience even when you do not feel it. Know that human emotions often lag intellect. We know [intellectually] we are commanded by Jesus to forgive even when we do not emotionally feel like doing it. Just do it [decide to speak it out loud] as a conscious and obedient act of your will. Over time, the Holy Spirit will reconcile your emotions and bring you peace.

There are positive benefits of speaking forgiveness **out loud.** In spiritual law [*sowing and reaping*], when you send out the positive energy of love and forgiveness into the universe you will begin to attract positive people, things, and circumstances back into your life over time. You are usually the first one to be blessed when you forgive, whether the other person deserves it or not.

When Jesus taught His disciples how to pray, He included forgiveness as a vital part of prayer. In the Lord's Prayer [Matthew 6:10-13] we are instructed to ask God for forgiveness as we forgive those who have wronged us. Jesus then goes into more detail about forgiveness in Matthew 14 and 15. Know that God will forgive a repentant sinner who asks for forgiveness, but on the condition that they also forgive anyone who has sinned against them. Basically, if you do not forgive, God will not forgive you.

This begs an important theological question: If you do not forgive and God does not forgive you, does this mean that you will go to hell (not heaven) because of your unrepented sin of unforgiveness? Repentance of sin is a big deal to God throughout scripture in the Bible.

Ephesians 6:12 tells us that we do not wrestle [battle] against flesh and blood [people] but against rulers of darkness [Satan and his demons]. It is important to realize that Satan is your real enemy, not people or God. People are simply tools, either in the hand of God for good to bless other people or in the hand of Satan to do his evil works and hurt other people.

Here is a simple analogy for you to consider: A hammer is a tool that can be used to either build up or tear down depending on the hand and heart of its user. It makes no sense to become either emotionally happy or angry at the hammer because it is only a tool. Realize that Satan is the evil operator in this world and people are his tools he uses for the destruction of God's people.

I once heard this saying that I believe to be true: *"Most problems in this world are caused by someone trying to feel important."* Modern examples of this concept include Putin, Hitler, Stalin, Pol Pot, Sadam

Hussein, etc. These wicked people were all tools [pawns] of Satan that he used to *steal, kill, and destroy* the lives of millions of innocent people.

When something good happens to you, give God the credit and glory. When bad things happen to you, blame Satan and take your God-given authority over him to cast him out.

It is easier to forgive people when you realize that they are only tools [pawns] that Satan uses when he can. Be angry at Satan and forgive people as Jesus commands.

My obedience level to this command is:

33. Don't be greedy or covetous

Luke 12:15   Then He said to them, *"Watch out and guard yourselves against every form of greed; for not even when one has an overflowing abundance does his life consist of nor is it derived from his possessions."*

Commentary on What to Know and Do:

Be on guard against every form of greed. Know that there is more to living a blessed and happy life than just having money and an abundance of possessions. Wealth cannot prolong man's natural life, avoid disease and avoid death. Do not covet [desire] what someone else might have that you do not. Guard your heart against futile pursuits. Ps 37:16 tells us "the little that a righteous man has is better than the riches of many wicked." The meaning of your life and the quality of your life are not measured by your wealth. Beware of chasing riches for the sake of trying to find meaning and contentment through wealth and possessions. Praise God and be genuinely happy for others who are blessed.

Know that comparing yourself to others causes major problems in your life. Learn to be grateful and content with what you have, versus fretting over what you do not [yet] have. Do not covet someone else's blessings or resent them for it.

My obedience level to this command is:

34. Honor Marriage

Matthew 19:6 *"So they are no longer two, but one flesh, therefore, what God has joined together, let no one separate."*

Matthew 19:9 *"I say to you, whoever divorces his wife, except for sexual immorality, and marries another woman commits adultery."*

Commentary on What to Know and Do:

View the bond of marriage as a sacred institution created by God Himself. The bond of marriage ought not to be dissolved by any man/woman or by any state, government or institution. It is not to be changed or altered by man at his whim or pleasure. Marriage is a sacred affair of God and not just a civil matter. In the institution of marriage, two people are so closely united together that they become as one flesh and one body. Let no man break the bond of union and dissolve the relationship for every trivial thing or upon any slight occasion.

Know that sexual immorality [including adultery] is listed in scripture as the only grounds for divorce.

Jesus was and is very clear on the sanctity of marriage and this verse is often quoted in wedding ceremonies: *"What God has brought together, let no one separate."* Honor the institution and sacrament of marriage.

My obedience level to this command is:

35. Lead by being a servant

Matthew 20:26-28   *"It is not this way among you* [the tyrannizing authority and power of the gentiles over other people], *but whoever wishes to become great among you shall be your servant and whoever wishes to be first among you shall be your* [willing and humble] *slave, just as the Son of Man did not come to be served, but to serve, and to give His life as a ransom for many* [paying the price to set them free from the penalty of sin].

Commentary on What to Know and Do:

Strive to be a servant leader. Jesus established the counter-intuitive principle for attaining greatness as being a "servant."

Have the view and attitude that you exist to serve others rather than to be served by others. Know that the value system in the Kingdom of God is a polar opposite of the carnal world in which we live. It is counter-intuitive, as are many other spiritual principles. Jesus plainly said that to be GREAT you must be a servant of others.

There is a cliche that says, "The greatness of a man is measured not by how many serve him, but rather by how many he serves."

Here are two very practical things you [as an obedient Christian] can do to demonstrate your servant's heart to other people.

1. Ask everyone "What can I do to help you?" And then do it.
2. Ask everyone "Is there anything I can pray about for you, your family or any of your friends?" And then do it. If they say yes, then have the guts to lay your hand on their shoulder and pray for what they asked right then and there.

God looks more at your heart attitude [motive] more than your results. Be sure your motives to serve others are pure by NOT expecting anything in return. God knows what you do and why you do it.

Jesus was the perfect example of a servant, of whom we are to emulate. Shortly before His arrest and execution, Jesus washed each of His disciples' feet. In Jewish society, this was the job of a household servant. Jesus, King of the Universe, humbled Himself unto death by washing the dirty feet of men. Are you a humble servant?

My obedience level to this command is:

36. Make the church a house of prayer for all nations

Mark 11:17   He began to teach and say to them, *"Is it not written, 'MY FATHER'S HOUSE SHALL BE CALLED A HOUSE OF PRAYER FOR ALL THE NATIONS'? But you have made it a ROBBER'S DEN."*

Commentary on What to Know and Do:

Keep the church focused and dedicated to worshiping God. Use the church for what it was intended. Do not let it become purely a social club more focused on making business contacts or conducting commerce. Welcome all God-worshipers of all economic levels, nationalities and races.

Do not ignore your responsibility for the needy, physically challenged, the elderly and widows. Do not choose expediency, commerce and convenience over the Gospel and caring for other people.

Here is a cliched statement worth keeping top-of-mind: "A church should be a hospital for sinners rather than a museum for saints." It is the hurting and sinful people who need the love of Jesus the most. Church members need to love the unlovable by sharing the

Gospel of Jesus, leading sinners to repentance, and making disciples of Christ Jesus.

Three of Jesus' parables tell us that heaven rejoices more over the repentance of one sinner more than 99 saints. Luke 15:4-7 the lost sheep, Luke 15:8-10 the lost coin, and Luke 15:12-31 the prodigal son

Be sure you obey Jesus' command concerning the role of His church and your role as a member of that church.

My obedience level to this command is:

37. Pray in faith (don't doubt)

Matthew 21:21-22   Jesus replied to them [about the withered fig tree], *"I assure you and most solemnly say to you, if you have faith [personal trust and confidence in Me] and do not doubt or allow yourself to be drawn in two directions, you will not only do what was done to the fig tree, but even if you say to this mountain, 'Be taken up and thrown into the sea,' it will happen [if God wills it]."*

"And whatever you ask for in prayer, believing, you will receive."

John 15:7-8   *"If you remain in Me and My words remain in you [that is, if we are vitally united and My message lives in your heart], ask whatever you wish and it will be done for you. My Father is glorified and honored by this, when you bear much fruit, and prove yourselves to be My [true] disciples."*

Commentary on What to Know and Do:

Do you believe and trust what Jesus told his disciples about prayer? Fundamentally He said believe without doubt and you will receive. The NLT says "You can pray for anything, and if you have faith, you will receive it." Know that the Bible gives conditions for answered prayer and they are intertwined: we must have faith, ask in Jesus' Name, and it must be according to God's will. Prayer is answered most often when these things come into alignment. This will happen more and more to one who seeks the face of God in close relationship, walks by His Spirit, surrenders his life to God and strives to do His will.

Know that in Biblical time the term "mountain" was used figuratively to represent problems or difficulties in one's life. Remember that much of Judea was mountainous with rocky difficult paths for travel. Jesus tells us to take authority [given to us by Him] over our problems [mountains] and command them to be changed for the better [thrown into the sea].

Prior to Jesus' death, He told His disciples to *"have faith and do not doubt."* Obviously, they were concerned and even afraid themselves. Jesus spoke His words of encouragement to them, but know that those words still apply to you and me today as Believers. If you trust that Jesus loves you and that God is sovereign and has a divine plan, there is no need for fear and doubt.

Ask yourself this question: "Do I make my choices and decisions based on faith or fear?" Fear is the sinful opposite of faith. Living a life based on faith (versus fear) allows you to be at peace and produce much *fruit* for the Kingdom of God.

Do you believe that you have God-given authority and that there is power in your spoken words? Jesus tells us that we do and He commands us to use it to *bear [produce] much fruit* so that the Father is glorified and honored.

When you are obedient to walk in this power, demonstrating your faith, and bearing much fruit, you are proving yourself to be His disciple [follower].

My obedience level to this command is:

38. Bring in the poor, invite the outcast

Luke 14:12-14   Jesus went on to say to the one who had invited Him, *"When you give a luncheon or a dinner, do not invite your friends or your brothers or your relatives or wealthy neighbors, otherwise they may also invite you in return and that will be your repayment."*

"But when you give a banquet or a reception, invite the poor, the disabled, the lame, and the blind and you will be blessed because they cannot repay you; for you will be repaid at the resurrection of the righteous [the just and the upright]."

Commentary on What to Know and Do:

We are commanded to provide care and extend hospitality to others without discrimination and without expecting future favors in return. Have pure motives in blessing others with your generosity when you have a party, feast or social function. It's OK to host friends and family, but be aware of your motives of expecting reciprocal treatment. Jesus urges us to Invite those who cannot repay you: the poor, the maimed, the lame, the blind. Know that you will be repaid and blessed in Heaven at the resurrection of the just. Be on guard when you host or attend a social function that your sole motivation is to be invited to some future function where you will receive reciprocal favors. Beware of this self-serving and selfish motive.

Jesus regularly demonstrated that he had a loving heart for the poor and the marginalized in the society of His day. We are commanded to have the same unselfish heart attitude and then to act on it. Jesus tells us there will be rewards in our afterlife for doing this. Loving other people is sometimes defined as "having an unselfish concern for the needs and well-being of others and then unselfishly acting on it to meet their needs."

My obedience level to this command is:

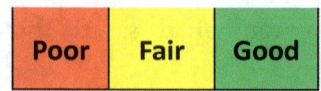

39. Render unto Caesar

Matthew 22:17, 19-21   Tell us [the disciples to Jesus] then, what do You think? 'Is it permissible [according to Jewish law and tradition] to pay a poll-tax to Caesar or not?

"Show me the coin used for the poll-tax." And they brought Him a denarius [a day's wage] and He said to them *"Whose likeness and inscription is this?"* They said "Caesar's [the Roman emperor Tiberius]" Then He said to them, *"Then pay to Caesar the things that are Caesar's; and to God the things that are God's."*

Malachi 3:10   Bring the full tithe into the storehouse, that there may be food in my house. And thereby, put me to the test, says the Lord of hosts, if I will not open the windows of heaven for you and pour down for you a blessing until there is no more need.

Commentary on What to Know and Do:

Basically, we are commanded to pay our taxes to the government and pay our tithes and offerings to God and to our church. In this context the meaning is to "give back" to the government what belongs to the government [its money and services] and give back to God what belongs to Him. Remember that God owns it all and we are but stewards of what He entrusts to us. Even if we do not like our government, we use its money and services in our daily lives, so we are obligated to pay our taxes, just as the Jews were required to pay Rome/Caesar his tax and tribute or suffer the consequences. Giving a portion of your money back to God as commanded is a matter of trusting Him to multiply your finances and provide for your needs. It is also a form of worship.

Know that it is the first fruits of your labor [income] that you are to return to God with faith, joy and thanksgiving. God loves a cheerful giver. How you use your money is a key indicator of your faith and trust in God. It is your *first fruits* offerings and tithes [your first and best] cheerfully given that God multiplies. God can do more with your tithe and offerings to bless you than you can do with 100% of your income. The Bible tells us in Malichi 3:10 to test and trust God in this. This is the only place in the Bible you are directed to test God [with your money].

Jesus tells you to respect the authority of the leaders over us and to obey public laws, whether you like them or not [like paying taxes]. I know far too many people who claim to be Christians who cheat to a greater or lesser degree on their income taxes. A better attitude to have is to give thanks to the Lord for providing the income that allows you to pay your taxes and enjoy the many blessings you have in the United States of America, One Nation Under God.

An old saying is "Give until it hurts." This is a wrong heart attitude [motive]. God is constantly looking at your motive [heart attitude] more than your results. A far better heart attitude is "Give until it feels good." This puts the spiritual law of giving and receiving *[sowing and reaping]* into motion for you.

Here is blunt analogy as food for thought. When you go into a store, you bring your money and exchange it for some desirable item, like a shirt. If you took the item but did not pay for it, you would be guilty of "shoplifting." Many people ask God for His blessings and enjoy the many services our government provides [peace, freedom, protection by the military, law and order, police, fire department, safety, security, electricity, water, sewer, etc.]. Know that when you do not tithe or pay your taxes you are "shoplifting" from God and the government. Are you a shoplifter or not? Do you render unto Caesar what is Caesar's and unto God what is God's as Lord Jesus commands?

My obedience level to this command is:

40. Love the Lord

Matthew 22:36-38   [A legal expert in the law asked Jesus] Teacher, which is the greatest commandment in the Law? And Jesus replied to him, *"YOU SHALL LOVE THE LORD YOUR GOD WITH ALL YOUR HEART, AND WITH ALL YOUR SOUL, AND WITH ALL YOUR MIND. This is the first and greatest commandment."*

Commentary on What to Know and Do:

Love God with all you heart, soul and mind. Know that this is the greatest commandment. Make God, Jesus, and the Holy Spirit first place in your life above anyone or anything else. You demonstrate your love for God when you obey the commands of the Son, Christ Jesus.

My obedience level to this command is:

41. Love your neighbor

Matthew 22:39   *"The second* [greatest commandment] *is like it, 'YOU SHALL LOVE YOUR NEIGHBOR AS YOURSELF'* [that is, unselfishly seek the best or higher good for others]."

THE 50 COMMANDS OF JESUS

<u>Commentary on What to Know and Do:</u>

Love your neighbor just as you are to love yourself. Know that Jesus said this is the second greatest commandment. Christian love can be described as having an unselfish concern for the needs and well-being of others and then acting unselfishly to meet those needs.

There is an old saying that says *"You can never receive what you have never given."* This corresponds to the Biblical principle of *sowing and reaping* [giving and receiving in spiritual law]. Giving opens the way for receiving. If you want to be loved, you must first give love that is unselfish and demands nothing in return. When you are obedient to send out real love, real love will return to you. As you love your neighbor as commanded by Jesus, you become one with God and thus you are one with the love that belongs to you by divine right.

Okay, so what if you violate this command and don't walk in love [to love your neighbor as yourself]? Most unhappiness and sickness come from violating the law of love. If you walk in hate, anger, resentment and criticism [rather than love] you will be vibrating to those negative energies and will most likely attract them into your life in the forms of sickness and sorrow. Choose to love your neighbor as yourself. This is hard to do, but work constantly on it as commanded. The blessings of obedience [joy, love and peace] far outweigh the consequences of disobedience.

You get what you give. Give love.

My obedience level to this command is:

42. Be born again

John 3:5-7   Jesus answered *"I assure you and most solemnly say to you, unless one is born of the water and of the Spirit, he cannot [ever] enter the Kingdom of God. That which is born of the flesh [the physical is merely physical] and that which is born of the Spirit is spirit. Do not be surprised that I have told you that you must be born again [reborn from above-spiritually transformed, renewed, sanctified].*

Commentary on What to Know and Do:

When you are born again, Jesus gives you a chance to start life all over again. You must choose to be spiritually reborn (changed, regenerated, transformed) from your carnal human nature ["the flesh"] into which you were naturally born. This spiritual rebirth happens when you decide that you believe in your heart and profess Jesus as your Lord and Savior trusting in His atoning sacrifice to forgive your sins so you can be in right-standing with God and go to Heaven. You also believe in the Resurrection that ushered in the New Covenant.

Know that all people, with their original human sin-nature, are opposed to God and are disobedient to Him; thus, they cannot relate to a holy God. The only way for you to change your nature is to be reborn in the "Spirit of God " and receive Jesus' atoning sacrifice in faith through grace.

My obedience level to this command is:

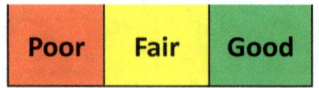

43. Await my return

Matthew 24:42-44   *"So be alert* [give strict attention, be cautious and active in faith], *for you do not know which day* [whether near or far] *your Lord is coming.*

But understand this: If the head of the house had known what time of the night the thief was coming, he would have been on his alert and would not have allowed his house to be broken into.

Therefore, you [who follow Me] *must also be ready; because the Son of Man is coming at an hour when you do not expect Him."*

Commentary on What to Know and Do:

Keep watch and stay on the lookout in anticipation of the return of the Lord. No one knows when this will happen, but we are to be prepared at all times and remain obedient to the commands of the Lord. Do not let your guard down because the Lord will come when you least expect Him. You never know when your earthly life is up, when the world [human life] may come to an end [via war or catastrophe], or when the Rapture may happen. Always be ready and qualified to go to your eternal home.

Human nature is pretty good at procrastinating. Do not put off getting your act together for God and in your trust and obedience to Christ Jesus. Be prepared and do it now, not later, lest it be too late. Know that if you miss the window and your name is NOT written in the Lamb's Book of Life, the consequences are not pretty.

My obedience level to this command is:

44. Celebrate the Lord's Supper

Matthew 26:26-28   Now as they were eating [the Passover meal] Jesus took bread, and after blessing it, He broke it and gave it to the disciples, and said, *"Take, eat; this is my body.* And when He had taken a cup and given thanks, He gave it to them saying, *"Drink from it, all of you; for this is my blood of the* [new and better] *covenant, which* [ratifies the agreement and] *is being poured out for many* [as a substitutionary atonement] *for the forgiveness of sins."*

Commentary on What to Know and Do:

Gladly participate in Holy Communion and celebrate your opportunity to do so with deep reverence. View the ritual as a remembrance of Jesus' last meal [also the Passover meal] with His disciples where He told them that he was offering his body and blood [tortured and crucified] on the next day for the benefit of humankind. Participate in remembering and taking the sacraments in a serious and worshipful frame of mind. Paul wrote that anyone who eats the bread or drinks the cup in an "unworthy" manner sins against Jesus and brings judgement on himself. Examine your heart attitude before taking the elements and focus on their true meaning and symbolism. Don't just go through the motions of the ritual. Jesus' command is simple: "Remember Me."

My obedience level to this command is:

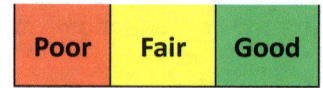

45. Watch and pray

Matthew 26:41   *"Keep actively watching and praying that you may not come into temptation; the spirit is willing, but the body is weak."*

Commentary on What to Know and Do:

Be constantly vigilant for the temptations Satan will throw at you. Pray that you are able to resist them. In our spirit we are willing to follow Jesus, but Satan knows our flesh is weak and he will attack us in many evil ways to try to get us away from God/Jesus. Be ready for this at all times and regularly pray for the strength to flee and resist all ungodly temptations that come your way.

You need to make an important decision in advance: that you will proactively avoid any situation that you could anticipate would provide a temptation for you to sin. If you find yourself in the midst of a temptation [or tempting situation], get up and leave [flee] immediately and do not look back lest you continue to be tempted.

My obedience level to this command is:

46. Keep my commandments

John 14:15   *"If you [really] love me, you will keep and obey My commandments."*

Commentary on What to Know and Do:

Knowing and obeying Jesus' commands is the primary way we show our love for Him. No one can claim to know and follow Christ while disregarding His teachings. True "born again" Christians don't make a habit of ignoring His teachings.

Know that the help and guidance of the Holy Spirit is vital for such obedience. The Holy Spirit will help bring Jesus' words and teaching to your recollection as needed. This presumes that you already have the words of Jesus implanted deeply in your mind and heart. Your role is to study, meditate and know Jesus' teachings and then to obey them. The Holy Spirit's role is to help you. Take and make time to do your part. Do you really love the Lord or just give it lip service? Is keeping and obeying Jesus' commands a priority in your life? If not, it should be.

My obedience level to this command is:

47. Feed my sheep (care for others)

John 21:15-16 *"Simon Peter, son of John, do you love me more than these* [others do, with total commitment and devotion]? He said to Him, "Yes, Lord; You know that I love You [with a deep, personal affection, as for a close friend]. Jesus said to him, *"Feed My lambs."*

Commentary on What to Know and Do:

We are to evidence our love for Jesus by caring for the "tender part of God's flock." This includes new believers, weak believers, and little children. We are to feed them with the "milk of the Gospel." Know that nothing has firmer and clearer proof and evidence of our love for Christ than to feed and take care of the "little lambs" of His flock.

Following Jesus' resurrection, He met with Peter on the beach. Peter had denied knowing Him three times prior to the crucifixion to protect himself. Jesus reconciles with Peter and then commanded him to *"Care for His sheep."*

Know that Jesus was delegating the responsibility to help care for believers to Peter as well as to the other disciples after He departed [ascended to heaven]. Today, that responsibility to care for others is delegated [commanded] to all believers in His church who claim to be disciples [followers] of Christ Jesus.

My obedience level to this command is:

48. Make and baptize disciples

Matthew 28:19 *"Go therefore and make disciples of all the nations* [help the people to learn of Me, believe in Me, and obey My words], *baptizing them in the name of the Father and of the Son and of the Holy Spirit."*

Commentary on What to Know and Do:

Go proactively into the world and teach people about the Gospel of Jesus. Also teach and explain to them the doctrines and the ordinances of the Gospel. We are to teach people by outwardly ministering the Gospel while the Spirit of God internally applies it. We are to baptize [dip] believers in water so they can outwardly demonstrate and proclaim their faith and belief in Jesus with their mouth and actions. Baptism is a symbolic death to self and being born again of the spirit. The water baptism is to be under the authority [in the name of] the Holy Trinity [Father, Son, and Holy Ghost]. Know that a disciple is a follower of a person and their teachings. As disciples of Jesus, we are to help make other disciples. Any believer has the authority to baptize someone; it is not limited just to ordained ministers.

Know that making a disciple [follower] of Jesus will take time and effort on your part. You assume the role of a teacher and mentor. Making a disciple is a process rather than a one shot and done. Consider setting a goal to make at least one disciple each year. It is a good start, and then go from there.

My obedience level to this command is:

49. Teach disciples to obey and keep Jesus' commandments

Matthew 28:20 *"Teach them to observe everything I have commanded you; and lo, I am with you always [remaining with you perpetually - regardless of circumstances, and on every occasion], even to the end of the age."*

Commentary on What to Know and Do:

Teach other disciples to know, obey and observe everything Jesus commanded. That includes things like: all ordinances [marriage, baptism, Lord's Supper, etc.], moral duties, and obligations to both men and God. Not only should disciples know the commands and have theory of them, but they should put them into practice. Also realize that Christ is with us to the end of the world, which goes beyond the end of our natural lives on earth. His spiritual presence [the Holy Spirit] remains to assist disciples in their work, to comfort them under all discouragements, to supply grace, and to protect them from enemies and evils. Remember that Jesus says, *"If you love me, keep my commandments."*

Again, here is an old saying: "If it doesn't make sense in the natural, it is probably from God."

Many times God will lead you to do things that don't always make sense in the natural [to your reasoning mind]. Remember that God's ways are not your ways and He will often direct you without sharing the "what and the why." Your role is to do what God says [be obedient] when He says to do it whether it makes any sense to you or not. God only asks you to obey Him instead of trying to reason everything out in your mind. The Bible is a book of over three-thousand promises for believers [you] if you will only receive them in faith and obedience. Know that there are many blessings for you in the spiritual principle of obedience.

A good Biblical example is when Jesus told Simon Peter [Luke 5:4-7] to let his nets down one more time after a long night of fishing with nothing caught. When Peter did as Jesus directed, his catch of fish was so large it nearly tore his nets and almost sunk his boat. God blessed Peter's obedience to Jesus' directive. This example still applies to us today. Know that your obedience to God's Word and commands leads to your blessings. God's ways are always better than our ways. Be sure to pray, listen and then obey.

Jesus clearly tells you in Luke 11: 28

"Blessed are those who hear the Word of God and keep it."

Teach others the important principle of hearing God's voice and then being promptly obedient without trying to reason everything to death. God responds to the faith, trust, and obedience of His sheep. You and I are directed to teach others the commands of Jesus and show them how to live and obey them.

My obedience level to this command is:

50. Receive God's power [and let it be your strength]

Luke 24:49   *"Listen carefully; I am sending the Promise of My Father* [the Holy Spirit] *upon you; but you are to remain in the city* [of Jerusalem] *until you are clothed [fully equipped] with power from on high."*

Commentary on What to Know and Do:

Ask for and seek God's power from on high in your life. This will enable you to be much more effective for the Lord than just trying to operate in your own limited human power. Let God's power be your strength. Jesus clearly told His disciples to wait in Jerusalem for the Baptism of the Holy Spirit before they attempted to preach the Gospel and minister to others.

Jesus told His followers in Matthew 28:18, *"All power is given unto me in heaven and earth."* Since He has ALL power, He has the authority to delegate that power to others including you and me. Jesus told His disciples [Luke 9:1] that He gave them power and authority over all demons and to cure diseases. Then Jesus looked at His other followers standing there and told them plainly [John 14:12-14],

12   *"I assure you and most solemnly say to you, anyone who believes in Me* [as Savior] *will do also the things I do, and he will do even greater things than these* [in extent and outreach], *because I am going to the Father."*

13   *"And I will do whatever you ask in My name* [as my representative], *this I will do that the Father may be glorified and celebrated in the Son,"*

14   *If you ask Me anything in My name* [as my representative], *I will do it."*

Know that Jesus' fame grew as He traveled throughout Judea teaching, healing and casting out demons. You and I are to do the same, but to an even greater degree.

You are to ask for the same power of God in your life. Know that it is available for all believers. The Spirit of God is a spirit of might, power, knowledge, understanding, wise counsel, love, sound mind, and courage to face the difficulties in this world as you faithfully proclaim the Gospel of Christ Jesus. Actively ask for and seek the "Baptism of the Holy Spirit." Then pray, listen, and obey the guidance of the Holy Spirit who is your Helper in all aspects of your life.

In the early 1900's, the great healing evangelist, Smith Wigglesworth, from Scotland was quoted as saying: "I am a thousand times more powerful on the inside than on the outside." He knew that the Holy Spirit dwelled within him and that the Holy Spirit was the source of great spiritual power. Wigglesworth knew it was God's power through the Holy Spirit that equipped and enabled him for great success and mighty healing miracles in his ministry. Wigglesworth knew he had no power in and of himself and that all spiritual power came from the Lord.

The early New Testament church grew rapidly because people witnessed many miracles [signs and wonders] and they were attracted to the visible **power** of God. Somehow, most churches today have ceased to walk in that power. It is God's will is for believers to walk in

His supernatural power. This includes power to overcome the world, the enemy and the flesh.

This begs an important question: *Is my church powerful or powerless?* You and I are directed to carry on Jesus' ministry on earth. The modern church needs to return to the point of God's POWER, operating in the power of the Word, the power of the Blood, and the power given us in the Holy Spirit.

Know that the same power from God is available to all believers for the asking. Surrender your will to God's will for you and ask for the Baptism of the Holy Spirit to come upon you. Walk in God's power [not your own] as you proclaim the Gospel of Jesus, produce good fruit, make disciples, and advance the Kingdom of God on earth. Know and be obedient to the commands of Christ Jesus.

My obedience level to this command is:

In Summary

As you study the teachings and commands of Jesus, you should notice that there are some important mega-themes that prevail:

- Stop sinning and truly repent
- Love God and people
- Treat people as you would like to be treated
- Forgive others
- Reconcile broken relationships
- Serve others
- Be generous
- Don't judge
- Rest in and trust in the goodness of God
- Fear not, be still [poised], and let God fight your battles [cast your burdens]

The Bible is a book with more than three-thousand promises for Believers. Contemporary author Steven K. Scott tells us in his book *"The Greatest Words Ever Spoken"* that there are 108 promises made by Jesus to Believers who choose to abide in His words. Scott's list of Jesus' promises includes the following blessings;

- You will receive eternal life
- Your desires will be fulfilled in answer to your prayers
- God the Father, Jesus and His Holy Spirit will be your constant companions, both with you and within you
- You will receive a level of peace and joy, direct from God, that is otherwise unattainable
- You will impact the lives of others in ways that can't be achieved strictly by human effort
- You will be loved by God in a unique way
- You will avoid God's ultimate judgement
- You will see miracles in your life that others can't understand or explain
- You will learn eternal truths that will set you free from all that holds you captive

Know that these promises and blessings are conditional and don't automatically manifest in everyone's life. They are available to those who believe in Christ Jesus and make a free-will choice to know His words and follow [obey] them.

Jesus' promises describe the condition that must be met [satisfied] and then the blessing that will follow. As you walk in Jesus' commands and study His promises, you will begin to see supernatural changes for the better show up in your life. Many times the supernatural changes in your life will defy what can be explained in the natural. Often, the manifestation will seem to be "too good to be true," but the evidence of it will amaze you.

I don't know about you, but I want all these promises and blessings to manifest in my life. I fully realize the blessings from God are contingent on my obedience to the Son's commands and teachings.

Just in case you haven't noticed, this book is about **"OBEDIENCE"** [duh]. Know that there are two kinds of obedience driven by two different sets of motives. The first is driven by "following rules" and the second is driven by "love." The first is a "got-to" motive and the second is a "want-to" motive. Remember that God looks deeply at your motives [heart] more than your results. God values your obedience [driven by love] more than your sacrifice. Consider which motive might drive you to follow the commands of Jesus.

I have a license plate holder on my car that says, "Jesus died for me, now I live for Him." It was His sacrificial love for you and me that led Him to the cross and kept Him there unto an agonizing human death. Hopefully, you will choose to love Him because He first loved you and paid the ultimate price for your blessings and salvation. Let your obedience be motivated by returning that great love to your Lord and Savior.

Pray that the Holy Spirit will give you an open heart to hear and understand Jesus' words and commands. Then pray for the desire to obey them wholeheartedly. Your obedience must be from the attitude of the heart and not just in in behavior only. Do whatever you do to honor and glorify God. Be obedient whether you feel like it or not and be quick to do whatever God directs you to do. As promised, a lifestyle of obedience will be rewarded. Never forget that God responds to and rewards those who seek Him diligently.

Personal Assessment

As you meditate on the teachings and commands of Christ Jesus as described in this book, ask yourself these questions:

Am I confident that I'm where I need to be in my Christian walk?

Where do I fall short in any of these commands?

What areas do I specifically need to work on to grow in my faith and obedience?

What are my priorities for self-development?

How should I go forward to develop the knowledge, belief, trust and obedience I need?"

If you have read these materials thus far, I can only assume you have a strong desire to be within the *will of God* for your life. As stated above, one of the best ways to be within the *will of God* is to study the life of Jesus, His decisions, behaviors and His teachings and commands. Take what you learn and apply those lessons daily in your life. Your Christian journey should involve becoming more like Jesus daily on your way to your eternal home in heaven.

If you are curious, you can calculate your overall "obedience score" in the following manner:

Count the number of times you rated your obedience level to each of the 50 commands as "red, yellow, or green" and enter those counts below. Multiply the count by the suggested point values and sum the points. Then divide by 50 (*) to get your overall obedience score on a 1-3 scale. Divide your Average Score by 3 and multiply by 100 to get your percentage score on a 0-100 scale. (like a numeric grade in school)

THE 50 COMMANDS OF JESUS

(*) Note: If you did not rate yourself on all 50 of the commands, but say you rated yourself on only 45 of the commands, then divide your total points by 45 to get the average.

# of REDS   _____   X 1 point = _____ points
# of YELLOWS   _____   X 2 points = _____ points
# of GREENS   _____   X 3 points = _____ points

    Total Points   _____ points
    Average Score   _____ points   (1 - 3 scale)
    Percentage Score _____%   (0 - 100 scale)

Percentage Score below 60 is   RED
Percentage score 60-84 is   YELLOW
Percentage score 85 and above is   GREEN

    Ask yourself: ***"How did I do and where do I need to improve to be more obedient to the Lord of my life?*** Again, making continuous progress should be the goal of a Christian.

    Suggestion: If you decide you want [need] to become more obedient to the Commands of Jesus, pick a limited number [one, two or three] of the commands and begin there. Determine what you currently think, say and do that is disobedient [either behaviorally or attitudinally] to the command and then pray for knowledge and wisdom from the Holy Spirit about what you need to think, say and do differently. Know that in self-development, it is usually more effective to work on only a few highly important changes at one time. Prioritize well and begin there.

Concluding thoughts:

The words of Jesus written in red can be the guiding *light* for your life so you do not have to stumble about and struggle in *darkness* on your journey to your eternal home. Make time to study the life and teachings of Jesus. Decide to make Him the **Lord** of your life as well as your **Savior** by learning His commands and then obeying them. You will be blessed and glad you did.

This book started with the corny statement "I hear ya' cluckin', but I don't see no eggs." As you become obedient to know and do the commands of Jesus, your life will produce an abundance of *good fruit* [eggs] for the kingdom of God. Hopefully, you will choose to truly make Jesus the **Lord** of your life rather to go through life just "cluckin'" about it.

As Apostle James reminds us in James 2:20 that *"faith without works* [action] *is dead."* In verse 18 James also said *"…I'll show you my faith by my works."* It is your faith in Jesus by God's grace that saves you [not your *works* alone], but your faith and obedience to Jesus' commands produce the *good fruit* that bring benefits and blessings to you and to the other people in your life.

In closing, I want to end this book with the lyrics from a contemporary song that just might surprise you. The lyrics are the chorus from the song *"Believe"* by the country-western duet Brooks and Dunn. They give sage advice for anyone claiming to be a Christian.

When I raise my hands, bow my head

I'm finding more and more truth in the words written in red

They tell me that there's more to life than just what I can see

I believe, oh I believe!

The 50 Commands of Christ Jesus
To Know and Obey (TKO)

(self-audit of your obedience)

Select a Time Period for this self-evaluation	Period Date Ending	Name: __
____ Day		Date this self-audit completed: ____
____ Week		
____ Month		
____ Year		

Question and food for thought: Do you <u>know</u> the commands of Jesus, and do you make a serious effort to <u>obey</u> them? (Or not?)

Jesus said these things (plus many others) about obeying His commnds:

"Those who accept my commands and obey them are the ones who love me. And because they love me, my Father will love them." John 14:21

"If you abide in me and my words abide in you, you can ask what you desire, and it shall be done for you. By this My Father is glorified that you bear much fruit." John 15:7-8 "Obey everything I have commanded you, and surely I am with you always, to the very end of the age." Matthew 28:20

"If you love me, you will obey what I command. And I will ask the Father, and he will give you another Counselor (Holy Spirit) to be with you forever." John 14:15-16

"… whoever does <u>not</u> obey the Son shall not see life, but the wrath of God remains on him." John 3:36 "Why do you call me 'Lord Lord' and do not do what I tell you?" Luke 6:46

"Blessed are those who hear the word of God and keep it." Luke 11:28

#	Commands of Jesus	Scripture(s)	Description of the Applied Behavior and What to Know	Self Evaluation of Your Obedience *(place an X in each row to rate yourself)*			
				Poor	Fair	Good	No Opportunity this period
1	**Repent (stop sinning)**	*Matt 4:17, Luke 13:3*	Turn your life around; stop sinning. Strive to think, say and do only things that please and honor God (not man). Have a Godly sorrow for your sin(s), confess them to God, ask for forgiveness, go a different/better direction in your life, don't repeat your sin(s), go forward constructively without guilt and shame. Rember that God judges' sin and there are consequences of your sins. The consequences are not always immediate because God loves you and patiently gives you time to change (repent). The consequences of your sins can carry on to your family through generational curses. Know that your sins rarely affect just you.				
2	**Let not you heart be troubled**	*John 14:1, 27, 33 Matt 6:25-26, Phil 4:6-7*	Be at peace and do not be afraid. There is no need to struggle with so many worries. Know that Jesus will bring a supernatural peace to believers that defies the world view of peace. Know that only Jesus can calm the storms of your life and bring you peace despite your circumstances Because of His love for us, we do not need to be troubled and worry if we will only abide in His Words, obey them, trust, and depend on Him. Jesus said the world will always be full of trouble, but he said to take heart because He has overcome the world. Take Jesus' yoke upon you and let Him carry your burdens. He will do that for you. Don't worry; be happy.				

#	Commands of Jesus	Scripture(s)	Description of the Applied Behavior and What to Know	Self Evaluation of Your Obedience *(place an X in each row to rate yourself)*			
				Poor	Fair	Good	No Opportunity this period
3	Follow Me	Matt 4:19	Follow Jesus' examples and learn from Him. Be mentored by Jesus by learning his words, thoughts, choices, and actions in daily living. Then emulate Him in your life based on what you learn from Him. Know and obey His commands by applying them in your daily life. Become a disciple and know that disciples help make other disciples. He told his disciples they would become "fishers of men." Are you a "fisher of men" who leads others to the Lord?				
4	Rejoice (be happy if others put you down)	Matt 5:10-12 2 Cor 12:10, James 1:2-4	Know and be glad that there is a great reward in Heaven for those who suffer "for righteousness, for Christ." (Followers of Jesus). Throughout history the speakers of unwelcomed truths (the prophets) were persecuted, and you will be persecuted too as a disciple of Christ Jesus. Be strong in your faith and be joyful knowing that great eternal rewards await you. Delight in your trials and persecutions knowing that when you are weak, that is when Christ is strong in you and for you. Be joyful knowing that trials in your life produce perseverance plus eternal rewards.				
5	Let your light shine	Matt 5:16	Become known for your goodness to others. Let your life light shine so all people can see your good works and praise/glorify your Father in Heaven. Walk in love, kindness, forgiveness, and mercy. Always do the right things right so your life is a living example for others.				

#	Commands of Jesus	Scripture(s)	Description of the Applied Behavior and What to Know	**Self Evaluation of Your Obedience** *(place an X in each row to rate yourself)*			
				Poor	Fair	Good	No Opportunity this period
6	Honor God's law	Matt 5:17-19	Know that Jesus came to fulfill the Law, not abolish, or change it. We are to follow the commandments of the Law and teach others to do so as well. There are great rewards in Heaven for doing this. You will be called 'great' in the Kingdom of God. Do not ignore God's Laws or lead others in not following the Laws and commandments. There are eternal penalties if you do this and you will be called 'least' in the Kingdom of God.				
7	Reconcile with your enemies	Matt 5:23-25	Don't bother coming to God with your gifts or petitions for your needs/wants before you have attempted to heal broken relationships with people. Go and reconcile with anyone you conflict with before you come to church seeking God. Often you must decide to forgive someone in your heart before you attempt to reconcile the relationship.				
8	Do not commit adultery or lust	Matt 5:27-29	Do not lust after or have relations with someone who is not your partner/spouse. You also commit adultery in your heart if you have a lustful eye. Resist temptation and do not let lust or sexual sin cast you into hell.				
9	Keep your word	Matt 5:33-37	Do not swear any oaths at all. Do what you say you will, and do not make promises you will not or cannot keep. Fulfill to the Lord any vows you have made. In your communication, let a simple YES or NO affirm the issue or deny the issue. Let you YES be YES, and your NO be NO. A simple YES or NO is enough; anything beyond this is from the evil one.				

#	Commands of Jesus	Scripture(s)	Description of the Applied Behavior and What to Know	Self Evaluation of Your Obedience *(place an X in each row to rate yourself)*			
				Poor	Fair	Good	No Opportunity this period
10	Go above and beyond	Matt 5:40-42	Be willing do more than whatever someone asks of you and then do it.				
11	Turn the other cheek and love your enemies	Matt 5:39, 5:44	Don't retaliate or take revenge on those who do you wrong. Don't repay evil for evil but trust in God's justice. This takes a lot of faith and patience. Pray blessings on your enemies and know that you will be the first to be blessed by God. Know that God's justice is always better than our revenge; however, God's timing for His justice may not always be the timing we would hope for.				
12	Be perfect (walk holy and be sinless)	Matt 5:48 Lav 19:2	Be perfect as your Father in Heaven is perfect. Strive to eliminate all conscious sin from your life and walk holy before our holy God. Aspire to live with the same kind of generosity and graciousness God directs toward us, His creation.				
13	Practice secret disciplines (giving, praying, fastings)	Matt 6:1-8	Don't show off your generosity. When you give to others don't make a fuss over it. Do your good deeds in private. God always knows what you did, and he values your unselfish heart attitude (motives). Strive to please God, not men.				

| | | | | Self Evaluation of Your Obedience | | | |
| | | | | *(place an X in each row to rate yourself)* | | | |
#	Commands of Jesus	Scripture(s)	Description of the Applied Behavior and What to Know	Poor	Fair	Good	No Opportunity this period
14	**Lay up treasures in heaven**	*Matt 6:19-21* *Luke 6:38* *Luke 16:10-12*	Invest in things that matter eternally, like the welfare of other people. Know that the acquisition of earthly wealth and possessions is "short-sighted." Seek to deploy your time and energies in advancing the Kingdom of God as the Holy Spirit directs you daily. Praise God regularly and be a blessing to as many people as you can every day.				
15	**Seek first the kingdom of God**	*Matt 6:33*	Seek first a personal relationship with God and then trust Him to provide for your needs because He loves you. Know that believers are adopted into His family and, as an heir, you are entitled to God's benefits. (Described well in Ps 103) Do not be consumed with worry about what you will eat drink or wear. Know that God is your provider. Keep God first place in your life. If Jesus' words abide in you and you abide (stay, dwell, rest, relax) in them, all things you need will be provided.				

#	Commands of Jesus	Scripture(s)	Description of the Applied Behavior and What to Know	Self Evaluation of Your Obedience *(place an X in each row to rate yourself)*			
				Poor	Fair	Good	No Opportunity this period
16	**Don't judge others, Judge not**	*Matt 7:1-2*	Know that it is God's role to judge people and not our role. Also know that if we judge others, God will judge us by the same standards we have applied. Work hard to resist the temptation to judge other people. If you are judgmental, you will be judged by God with the same measure you have applied.				
17	**Do not throw your pearles to pigs**	*Matt 7:6*	Do not persist in sharing your faith and the Gospel with people who do not wish to hear it. If you determine your message is unwelcome and totally rejected, be comfortable in just politely walking away. Do your best and then trust God for the rest. It is the Holy spirit's job to convict their heart, not yours. Trust God to do what you cannot do and then be at peace about it.				

				Self Evaluation of Your Obedience *(place an X in each row to rate yourself)*			
#	Commands of Jesus	Scripture(s)	Description of the Applied Behavior and What to Know	Poor	Fair	Good	No Opportunity this period
18	Ask, seek, knock	Matt 7:7-8	When you pray, ask God for wisdom and to meet your daily needs. Trust Him to be your provider and protector. Realize He will do this because He loves you and has adopted you as a Believer into His family. When you ask, seek, and knock, it honors and pleases God when you surrender and acknowledge your dependence on Him. Remember that Jesus loves to answer your prayers and to give you what you seek so that your joy may be made full.				
19	Treat others as you would like to be treated, Do unto others	Matt 7:12	Treat others in the same good manner you would like to be treated. This is commonly called the Golden Rule. Know that when you think, say, and do good deeds to bless others, you are putting the principles of love and sowing and reaping into action. In spiritual law "like energies attract like energies." You will attract similar good things back into your life.				

#	Commands of Jesus	Scripture(s)	Description of the Applied Behavior and What to Know	Self Evaluation of Your Obedience *(place an X in each row to rate yourself)*			
				Poor	Fair	Good	No Opportunity this period
20	**Choose the narrow way**	*Matt 7:13-14*	Know that there are two different interpretations of this command. The common interpretations say there are two paths/gates: one leads to Heaven and the other leads to Hell (the two destinies that await humanity). The path to Heaven is narrow and difficult, not many people will choose this gate. Only a few will find it and go in. Those few believe in and follow Jesus in faith calling Him Lord and obey His commands. The path to Hell is broad and easy and it attracts many people to it.				

#	Commands of Jesus	Scripture(s)	Description of the Applied Behavior and What to Know	Self Evaluation of Your Obedience *(place an X in each row to rate yourself)*			
				Poor	Fair	Good	No Opportunity this period
20	**Choose the narrow way** *(continued) from the previous page*	*Matt 7:13-14*	Those who choose this route are bound for destruction and Hell because they have rejected Jesus and choose not to believe He is the only path to salvation. A less common interpretation applies only to Christians. There is a spiritual gateway and a carnal gateway. The spiritual path leads to abundant and victorious life, and the carnal path results in the loss of reward for a wasted and defeated life. The spiritual path requires true disciples to have discipline, dedication, and death to self. The carnal path results in a life without meaning; a wasted life where Christ was not central, and God was not glorified.				
21	**Beware of false prophets**	*Matt 7:15*	Look for and do not be fooled by a "wolf in sheep's clothing." This can apply to those who claim to be religious leaders, prophets, and make false religious claims. They are deceptive and dangerous. A religious leader may appear to be wise and respectable, but you must look at the fruits of his life to know if he truly represents God and does the will of the Father.				

#	Commands of Jesus	Scripture(s)	Description of the Applied Behavior and What to Know	Self Evaluation of Your Obedience *(place an X in each row to rate yourself)*			
				Poor	Fair	Good	No Opportunity this period
22	**Pray for more helpers (who help spread the Word)**	*Matt 9:37-38*	Pray to the Lord who oversees the harvest and ask Him to send more workers into His fields. Jesus saw many people who were ready to believe in Him but realized there were too few workers to go out to the masses ready to be harvested. Jesus asks His followers today to participate in the solution to this problem. We are to pray and send, or to go ourselves.				
23	**Be wise and inoffensive**	*Matt 10:16, Rom 16:19*	Jesus empowered His disciples and gave them specific instructions to preach, heal the sick and to proclaim the kingdom of God. He told them to take care because He was sending them into a world ruled by Satan. Like the disciples, we are to be wise as to what is good and innocent versus what is evil. Today, we are to preach, heal and proclaim the Gospel as we also apply wisdom concerning the evil world into which we are sent.				

#	Commands of Jesus	Scripture(s)	Description of the Applied Behavior and What to Know	Self Evaluation of Your Obedience *(place an X in each row to rate yourself)*			
				Poor	Fair	Good	No Opportunity this period
24	**Fear God, do not fear man**	*Matt 10:28, Luke 12:4-5*	Do not fear man who can only kill your body but not your soul. Instead fear (reverence, great and profound respect) God who can both kill your body and condemn your soul to Hell. Know that the death of the body is not the ultimate loss, but the death of the body and the soul together in Hell are the ultimate loss.				
25	**Listen to God's voice**	*Matt 11:15, 13:9, 13:43, Mark 4:23, Luke 14:35*	When God speaks something important to us, we are to listen carefully. "He who has ears, let him hear." Some teachings (like the parables) require us to listen carefully and interpret them with more than just ordinary powers of speech and words. We are to give the highest attention to what was spoken by Jesus, take it in deeply and remember it. Take head of what you hear. The more you hear, the more will be shared. Do not let you ears become hard of hearing and your heart grow hard to God's voice. Know that God often speaks to us through His Word and that "still small voice."				

				Self Evaluation of Your Obedience *(place an X in each row to rate yourself)*			
#	Commands of Jesus	Scripture(s)	Description of the Applied Behavior and What to Know	Poor	Fair	Good	No Opportunity this period
26	**Cast your burdens onto Him (take my yoke)**	*Matt 11:28-30*	Know that when we choose to become "yoked" with Jesus, He will guide and direct our lives in ways that make our lives easier and bring peace and rest to our souls (minds). His yoke is easy, and His burden is light. His commandments are not burdens on us but rather guide us into God's will for our lives and blessings begin to flow. Going God's way brings rest to our souls; going our own way in life will never bring rest. Let the God of peace have full control over your life. Be happy to be "yoked" to Jesus.				
27	**Honor your parents**	*Matt 15:4-7*	Honor, respect and obey your parents. If you curse them, there may be bad and negative consequences in your life, both in the natural and in the spiritual. Do not speak evil of your parents. Take care of them in their old age and/or infirmity.				
28	**Beware of false teaching**	*Matt 16:6, 11-12*	Beware of the yeast of the Pharisees. Know that yeast was often a metaphor for evil in Jewish teaching. Be on guard against teachers who teach false doctrines and ideas. Following those wrong ideas can lead to enormously wrong beliefs. Test and compare all teaching you hear against the Word of God, the Bible. Beware if there is little or no alignment.				

#	Commands of Jesus	Scripture(s)	Description of the Applied Behavior and What to Know	Self Evaluation of Your Obedience *(place an X in each row to rate yourself)*			
				Poor	Fair	Good	No Opportunity this period
29	**Deny yourself**	*Luke 9:23, Matt 10:38, Mark 8:34*	Choose to love Jesus more than anyone else (including family) and live for Him alone. Be willing to let go of your own personal agendas, desires, wishes, dreams, and ways of living to walk the difficult path of Christ fully submitted to the will of God for you and your life. Know that those who follow Jesus will find the life that is true and those who go their own way will lose their lives, no matter what they find on earth. Be so willing to deny yourself that you are willing to die for Christ.				
30	**Do not despise little ones**	*Matt 18:10*	See that you do not look down on, despise or think less of any of the little children. Know that their angels in heaven always see the face of the Father who is in heaven.				

#	Commands of Jesus	Scripture(s)	Description of the Applied Behavior and What to Know	Self Evaluation of Your Obedience *(place an X in each row to rate yourself)*			
				Poor	Fair	Good	No Opportunity this period
31	**Go directly to Christians who offend you**	*Matt 18:15, Gal 6:1*	If a fellow Christian brother wrongs you by either their words or actions, you should not complain of it to others. Instead, you should go directly to them in private to state the matter kindly, show him (describe) his conduct and explain its negative impact. Press it home in such a way to reach his reason and consciousness. If he listens to you, you have won a brother. Know that a little friendly conversation can often set the matter straight and avoid further difficulty. Today, too few people take this commanded direct approach. Many people would welcome the opportunity of acknowledging their wrong conduct and making it right. It is our obligation to furnish them with the opportunity. Remember that angry words spoken in front of others often fail to reach the desired outcome. In life it is best to "praise publicly and criticize privately."				

| | | | | Self Evaluation of Your Obedience |||||
| | | | | *(place an X in each row to rate yourself)* |||||
#	Commands of Jesus	Scripture(s)	Description of the Applied Behavior and What to Know	Poor	Fair	Good	No Opportunity this period
32	**Forgive offenders**	*Matt 6:12, 6:14-15, 18:21 Prov 19:11*	We are commanded to forgive people who offend us or do us wrong an unlimited number of times. It often takes wisdom, patience, and obedience to overlook the offences of others. Know that we will not be forgiven of our offenses (sins) unless we forgive others. Peter asked Jesus about forgiving someone 7 times in a day, and Jesus told him 70 X 7, which really means an unlimited number of times. Know that there are negative consequences to unforgiveness. When we walk in constant unforgiveness, we open spiritual and physical doorways for problems, sickness, and disease to manifest in our lives. Speak forgiveness out loud through an act of obedience even when you do not feel it. Over time, the Holy Spirit will reconcile your emotions and bring you peace.				

#	Commands of Jesus	Scripture(s)	Description of the Applied Behavior and What to Know	Self Evaluation of Your Obedience *(place an X in each row to rate yourself)*			
				Poor	Fair	Good	No Opportunity this period
33	**Don't be greedy, don't covet**	*Luke 12:15*	Be on guard against every form of greed. Know that there is more to living a blessed and happy life than just having money and an abundance of possessions. Wealth cannot prolong man's natural life, avoid disease, and avoid death. Do not covet (desire) what someone else might have that you do not. Guard your heart against futile pursuits. Ps 37:16 tells us "The little that a righteous man has is better than the riches of many wicked." The meaning of your life is not measured by your wealth. Beware of chasing riches for the sake of trying to find meaning and contentment through riches and possessions. Praise God and be genuinely happy for others who are blessed.				

| | | | | Self Evaluation of Your Obedience | | | |
| | | | | *(place an X in each row to rate yourself)* | | | |
#	Commands of Jesus	Scripture(s)	Description of the Applied Behavior and What to Know	Poor	Fair	Good	No Opportunity this period
34	**Honor marriage**	*Matt 19:6, 19:9*	View the bond of marriage as a sacred institution created by God Himself. The bond of marriage ought not to be dissolved by any man/woman or by any state, government, or institution. It is not to be changed or altered by man at his pleasure. Marriage is a sacred affair of God and not just a civil matter. In the institution of marriage, two people are so closely united together that they become as one flesh and one body. Let no man break the bond of union and dissolve the relationship for every trivial thing or upon any slight occasion.				
35	**Lead by being a servant**	*Matt 20:26-28*	Strive to be a servant leader. Have the view and attitude that you exist to serve others rather than be served by others. Know that the value system in the Kingdom of God is an opposite of the carnal world in which we live. It is counterintuitive. Jesus plainly said that to be GREAT you must be a servant of others. He was the perfect example, of which we are to emulate.				

#	Commands of Jesus	Scripture(s)	Description of the Applied Behavior and What to Know	Self Evaluation of Your Obedience *(place an X in each row to rate yourself)*			
				Poor	Fair	Good	No Opportunity this period
36	**Make the church a house of prayer for all people**	*Mark 11:17*	Keep the church focused and dedicated to worshiping God. Do not let it become purely a social club more focused on making business contacts or conducting commerce. Welcome all God-worshipers of all economic levels, nationalities, and races. Do not ignore our responsibility for the needy, physically challenged, the elderly and widows. Do not choose expediency and convenience over the gospel.				
37	**Pray in faith without doubt**	*Matt 21:21-22, John 15:7-8*	Do you believe and trust what Jesus told his disciples about prayer? Fundamentally He said believe and receive. The NLT says, "You can pray for anything, and if you have faith, you will receive it." Know that the Bible gives conditions for answered prayer and they are intertwined: we must have faith, ask in Jesus' Name, and it must be according to God's will. Prayer is answered most often when these things come into alignment. This will happen more and more to one who seeks the face of God in close relationship, walks by His Spirit, surrenders his life to God and strives to do His will.				

#	Commands of Jesus	Scripture(s)	Description of the Applied Behavior and What to Know	Self Evaluation of Your Obedience *(place an X in each row to rate yourself)*			
				Poor	Fair	Good	No Opportunity this period
38	**Bring in the poor, invite the outcast**	*Luke 14:12-14*	We are required to afford care and hospitality toward others without discrimination and without expecting future favors in return. Have pure motives in blessing others with your generosity when you have a party, feast, or social function. It's OK to host friends and family but be aware of your motives of expecting reciprocal treatment. Jesus urges us to invite those who cannot repay you: the poor, the maimed, the lame, the blind. Know that you will be repaid and blessed in Heaven at the resurrection of the just. Be on guard when you host or attend a social function and your sole motivation is to be invited to some future function where you will receive reciprocal favors. Beware of this self-serving and selfish motive.				

#	Commands of Jesus	Scripture(s)	Description of the Applied Behavior and What to Know	Self Evaluation of Your Obedience *(place an X in each row to rate yourself)*			
				Poor	Fair	Good	No Opportunity this period
39	Render unto Caesar	Matt 22:17, 19-21 Mal 3:10	Basically, we are commanded to pay our taxes and pay our tithes and offerings to God and to our church. In this context the meaning is to "give back" to the government what belongs to the government (its money) and give back to God what belongs to Him. Remember that God owns it all and we are but stewards of what He gives us. Even if we do not like our government, we use its money and services in our daily lives, so we are obligated to pay our taxes, just as the Jews were forced to pay Rome/Caesar his tax and tribute or suffer the consequences. Giving a portion of our money back to God as commanded is a matter of trusting Him to multiply our finances and provide for our needs.				
40	Love the Lord	Matt 22:36-38	Love God with all you heart, soul, and mind. Know that this is the greatest commandment. Make God, Jesus, and the Holy Spirit first place in your life above anyone or anything else. You demonstrate your love for Jesus when you obey His commands.				

#	Commands of Jesus	Scripture(s)	Description of the Applied Behavior and What to Know	Self Evaluation of Your Obedience *(place an X in each row to rate yourself)*			
				Poor	Fair	Good	No Opportunity this period
41	**Love your neighbor**	*Matt 22:39*	Love your neighbor just as you are to love yourself. Know that Jesus said this is the second greatest commandment. Christian love can be described as having an unselfish concern for the needs and well-being of others and then acting unselfishly to meet those needs.				
42	**Be born again**	*John 3:5-7*	You must choose to be spiritually reborn (changed, regenerated, transformed) from your carnal human nature ("the flesh") into which you were naturally born. This spiritual rebirth happens when you decide that you believe in your heart and profess Jesus as your Lord and Savior trusting in His atoning sacrifice to forgive your sins so you can be in right-standing with God and go to Heaven. You also believe in the Resurrection that ushered in the New Covenant. Know that all people, with their original human sin-nature, are opposed to God and are disobedient to Him; thus, they cannot relate to a holy God. The only way for a person to change his nature is to be reborn in the "Spirit of God " and receive Jesus' atoning sacrifice in faith through grace.				

#	Commands of Jesus	Scripture(s)	Description of the Applied Behavior and What to Know	Self Evaluation of Your Obedience (place an X in each row to rate yourself)			
				Poor	Fair	Good	No Opportunity this period
43	**Await my return**	*Matt 24:42-44*	Keep watch and stay on the lookout in anticipation of the return of the Lord. No one knows when this will happen, but we are to be always prepared and remain obedient to the commands of the Lord. Do not let your guard down because the Lord will come when you least expect Him.				
44	**Celebrate the Lord's Supper**	*Matt 26:26-28*	Gladly participate in Holy Communion and celebrate your opportunity to do so with deep reverence. View the ritual as a remembrance of Jesus last meal (also the Passover meal) with His disciples where He told them that he was offering his body and blood (crucified) on the next day for the benefit of humankind. Participate in remembering and taking the sacraments in a serious and worshipful frame of mind. Paul wrote that anyone who eats the bread or drinks the cup in an "unworthy" manner sins against Jesus and brings judgement on himself. Examine your heart attitude before taking the elements and focus on their true meaning and symbolism. Don't just go through the motions.				

| | | | | Self Evaluation of Your Obedience ||||
| | | | | *(place an X in each row to rate yourself)* ||||
#	Commands of Jesus	Scripture(s)	Description of the Applied Behavior and What to Know	Poor	Fair	Good	No Opportunity this period
45	Watch and pray	*Matt 26:41*	Be constantly vigilant for the temptations Satan will throw at you. Pray that you can resist them. In our spirit we are willing to follow Jesus, but Satan knows our flesh is weak and he will attack us in many evil ways to try to get us away from God/Jesus. Be always ready for this and regularly pray for the strength to flee and resist all ungodly temptations that come your way.				
46	Keep my commandments	*John 14:15*	Knowing and obeying Jesus' commands is the primary way we show our love for Him. No one can claim to know and follow Christ while disregarding His teachings. True "born again" Christians don't make a habit of ignoring His teachings. Know that the guidance of the Holy Spirit is key for such obedience.				
47	Feed my sheep	*John 21:15-16*	We are to evidence our love for Jesus by caring for the "tender part of God's flock." That includes new believers, weak believers, little children. We are to feed them with the "milk of the Gospel." Know that nothing has firmer and clearer proof and evidence of our love for Christ than to feed and take care of the "little lambs" of His.				

#	Commands of Jesus	Scripture(s)	Description of the Applied Behavior and What to Know	Self Evaluation of Your Obedience *(place an X in each row to rate yourself)*			
				Poor	Fair	Good	No Opportunity this period
48	Make and baptize disciples	Matt 28:19	Go proactively into the world and teach people about the Gospel of Jesus. Also teach and explain to them the doctrines and the ordinances of the Gospel. We are to teach men by outwardly ministering the Gospel while the Spirit of God internally applies it. We are to baptize (dip) believers in water so they can outwardly demonstrate and proclaim their faith and belief in Jesus with their mouth and actions. The water baptism is to be under the authority (in the name of) the Holy Trinity (Father, Son, and Holy Ghost). Know that a disciple is a follower of a person and their teachings. As disciples of Jesus, we are to help make other disciples. Any believer has the authority to baptize someone; it is not limited just to ordained ministers.				

#	Commands of Jesus	Scripture(s)	Description of the Applied Behavior and What to Know	Self Evaluation of Your Obedience *(place an X in each row to rate yourself)*			
				Poor	Fair	Good	No Opportunity this period
49	Teach disciples to obey Jesus' commandments	Matt 28:20	Teach other disciples to know, obey and observe everything Jesus commanded. That includes things like all ordinances (marriage, baptism, Lord's Supper, etc.), moral duties, and obligations to both men and God. Not only should disciples know the commands and have theory of them, but they should put them into practice. Also realize that Christ is with us to the end of the world, which goes beyond the end of our natural lives on earth. His spiritual presence (the Holy Spirit) remains to assist disciples in their work, to comfort them under all discouragements, to supply grace, and to protect them from enemies and evils.				

| | | | | Self Evaluation of Your Obedience | | | |
| | | | | *(place an X in each row to rate yourself)* | | | |
#	Commands of Jesus	Scripture(s)	Description of the Applied Behavior and What to Know	Poor	Fair	Good	No Opportunity this period
50	Receive God's power (let it be your strength)	Luke 24:49	Ask for and seek God's power from on high in your life. This will enable you to be much more effective for the Lord than just trying to operate in your own limited human power. Jesus clearly told His disciples to wait in Jerusalem for the Baptism of the Holy Spirit before they attempted to preach the Gospel and minister to others. You are to ask for the same power of God in your life. Know that it is available for all believers. The Spirit of God is a spirit of might, power, knowledge, understanding, wise counsel, love, sound mind and courage to face the difficulties in this world as you faithfully proclaim the gospel of Christ Jesus. Actively ask for and seek the "Baptism of the Holy Spirit." Then pray, listen, and obey the guidance of the Holy Spirit who is your Helper in all aspects of your life.				

> Determine your level of obedience to the commands of Jesus.

Count the # of X in each column for the Commands, i.e., # rated Poor, # rated Fair, # rated Good, # rated Not Applicable This Period. The total across should = 50 if you marked an X for each of the 50 Commands. Sum the count of X for your ratings of Poor, Fair, Good and record that sum in box (A) below.				
				(A)

	x 1 pt	x 2 pts	x 3 pts	x 0 pts
Calculate the # of Points for Each Rating (Poor, Fair, Good), Then sum the # points across the four columns and record the total in box (B) below				0
				(B)

Calculate Your Overall Avg. Score for Obedience to Jesus' Commands Divide the sum of all points (B) by the count of the # of applicable commands (A) you rated on the P, F, G scale, don't count the nos.	

				Self-Evaluation of Your Obedience (Place an **X** in each row to rate yourself)			
#	Commands of Jesus	Scripture(s)	Description of the Applied Behavior and What to Know	**Poor**	**Fair**	**Good**	No Opportunity this period

Interpretation of your Average Score for Obedience	Comment	
2.55 and above is Green/Good (85% to 100%)	Good job, keep it going	☺
1.80 to 2.54 is Fair/Yellow (60% to 84%)	Not bad, but you can do better	😐
1.79 and below is Poor/Red (59% and below)	You need to make a focused effort	☹

Determine and List Your Top 3 improvement goals	Command #	My Personal Action Plan for Improvement

www.ingramcontent.com/pod-product-compliance
Lightning Source LLC
La Vergne TN
LVHW022000060526
838201LV00048B/1638